ENDORSEMENT QUOTES

"This is a great read, drawing you in to the lives of women who persist in following their ambitions and passions and as they learn about themselves, grow more emboldened to take leaps and risks that result in greater and greater accomplishments. It is a wonderful portrayal of feminine power."

SUSAN RODRIGUEZ

"This anthology captures the quiet courage and hard-won wisdom of women who've redefined success for themselves, often more than once. It's not only a reflection of where we've been, but a resource and roadmap for daughters, mentees, and future leaders finding their own way."

BONNIE SOUTHCOTT

"If you've ever played pinball, you know that the ball can seem to aimlessly roll downward. Gravity pulls it but there's no way to know exactly *where* it will go. Like the pinball, each author had a career direction in mind only to find themselves landing in a spot or hitting a bumper that careened them in a different, exciting direction. Each one *kept moving*...kept pinging...and kept racking up points on the scoreboard of life. And even if the ball slipped passed a flipper, the game didn't end — they just pulled back on the lever and sent another ball out on its next adventure. Here's to pulling your lever and keeping the game going!"

MYLENE BARIZO

POWER OF WHAT'S NEXT

BOLD MOVES BY DESIGN

POWER OF WHAT'S

NEXT

BOLD MOVES BY DESIGN

NATALIE BENAMOU
HOPE MUELLER

DIANNE BOYER · WENDI O. BROWN · NANCY HEDLUND
JENNIFER PETERS · LIESL SCHMIDT · LAURIE WESSELS
JANET WINKLER · CYNDY WULFSBERG

POWER OF WHAT'S NEXT: BOLD MOVES BY DESIGN

Copyright © 2025 Hope Mueller, Hunter Street Press

All rights reserved. No part of this book may be reproduced, stored, or transmitted by any means—whether auditory, graphically, mechanically, or electronically—without written permission of the publisher. Unauthorized reproduction of any part of this work is illegal and is punishable by law.

ISBN: 978-1-967071-03-6 (Jacketed Hardcover)
ISBN: 978-1-967071-02-9 (eBook)

Published by Hunter Street Press

DEDICATION

This book is written with love and appreciation for my daughters, Arianna and Valentina, and my husband Sergio.

CONTENTS

Introduction 1
   The Windshield is Bigger than the Rear View Mirror....... 1

Introduction to Laurie Wessels 3
   Not Done Yet! 5

Introduction to Dianne Boyer 11
   Joy in the Mirror 13

Introduction to Janet Winkler 29
   Forget Grit. My Power Move
   Was Subtraction by Design. 31

Introduction to Cyndy Wulfsberg 43
   Do You Want to Tell a Story? 45

Introduction to Jennifer Peters 65
   Find Your Me-Suite 67

Introduction to Wendi O. Brown 83
   Profit Powerhouse 85

Introduction to Nancy Hedlund 101
   The Final Pivot 103

Introduction to Liesl Schmidt 125
   Moment of Purpose 127

Introduction to Natalie Benamou 141
   Fly Through the Window 143

Epilogue 159
Acknowledgements 161
Discussion Guide Questions 165

DISCLAIMER

This anthology is a work of non-fiction based on the each individual author's recollections of events, conversations, and experiences over time. While every effort has been made to present these accounts accurately and truthfully, some names, and identify details, and events may have been changed, condensed or reconstructed for narrative clarity and to protect individual privacy. The views and opinions expressed are solely those of each author and do not necessarily reflect this of the managing author, editor, or publisher. Any resemblance to real persons, living or dead, or actual events is purely coincidental and unintentional unless explicitly stated. All authors, editor and publisher disclaim any liability for any loss injury, or damages resulting form the content herein.

Each author has confirmed their contribution is their original work, is not produced by Artificial Intelligence, has not been previous published, and contains nothing which is libelous, in breach of any obligation of confidentiality or official acts or anything which would constitute a malicious falsehood or is otherwise unlawful; their contribution will not infringe the copyright, trademark, trade secret, right of privacy or publicity or any other rights of third party.

INTRODUCTION
THE WINDSHIELD IS BIGGER THAN THE REAR VIEW MIRROR

On a cold winter evening, I embarked on a familiar task: to find meaningful content to share with the Mastermind group that would meet later in the week. When asked what topic would be most helpful several expressed *staying relevant over fifty.*

This was not a new topic, we had discussed how women over fifty are often overlooked and that ageism was real. Two of the women in the cohort were exploring new careers over sixty and others were deciding when the right time was to exit their corporate roles.

As I researched the topic, what stood out was there wasn't any advice. In fact, the only article I could find, was fashion advice from a man. He suggested women over fifty should ask younger women for tips on how to, look younger and thereby stay relevant.

The lack of resources ignited a fire and I opened the Mastermind with the story of my research. There was a resounding chorus from all the women "We are not done yet!" One by one, they shared their stories and what it meant to them to be active, relevant, and contributing. Sometimes what we are searching for is right before us. It turned out we didn't need anyone to tell us how to remain relevant. We could define what that meant all on our own.

What started out as research, transformed into a movement and the group enthusiastically said they wanted to share their stories. Ever curious and an interviewer at heart, I started asking women what it meant to be relevant over fifty. Although each had a different take on the meaning, the through line was that not only were they not done yet, they were just getting started.

Through initial conversations, the authors in this anthology shared what it meant to her to be free to decide her destiny. Imagining what it could look like to boldly make moves on their own terms. It wasn't until I read each of their stories that I fully appreciated the magnitude and beauty of resilience, transformation and an unwavering fortitude to keep moving forward.

Our hope is to inspire women to believe that at any age, we have the power to define what's next. It is not that we don't know how to be relevant, we are creating a whole new definition on our terms. Be bold. Make your own moves. Live your life by design.

INTRODUCTION TO
LAURIE WESSELS

Laurie Wessels is a seasoned Senior Executive and Consultant with more than 40 years of success in the pharmaceutical, engineering, higher education, and executive coaching industries. Leveraging extensive experience with highly lucrative product launches and marketing in the pharmaceutical industry as well as in the design of coaching and training programs for an array of Fortune 500 companies, she is an asset for companies in the life sciences sector seeking expert advice in the areas of change management, relationship building, strategic decisions, and leader development.

Her broad areas of expertise include leadership development, executive coaching, change management, strategic planning, organizational development, program management, team building, sales, marketing, and instructional design.

Throughout her career, Laurie has held leadership positions at organizations including Wessels Group Inc., Pfizer, and Parke-Davis. As President of the Wessels Group since

2000, she leads services in executive development and strategic management. She is also a Faculty Member of The Global Institute for Leadership Development since 2007, Lake Forest Graduate School of Management since 2003, and Northwestern University since 2014. She previously had a 15-year career in the pharmaceutical industry as a Senior Marketing Manager with Parke-Davis Pharmaceuticals. She has been responsible for creating product strategies and tactics resulting in more than $3 billion in sales and was instrumental in the launch of the highly successful cholesterol drug Lipitor. She has designed coaching, mentoring, and leadership programs for numerous organizations. Laurie holds an MBA from Saint Ambrose University and holds several certifications in Executive Coaching and Leadership Development.

Not Done Yet!

I am the radiant sunlight rippling on the waves of transformation.

This Identity Statement, which I composed years ago, popped into my head as I watched the orange, yellow, and blue hues reflect on the Gulf of Mexico waters with the setting sun. I wrote the Identity Statement during a career change twenty-five years ago, representing how I wanted to show up in the world. My passion was to help others to be the best they could be.

Like the waves crashing on the beach, reality bashed into my brain. *What on earth does that mean? How will I ever do that?*

This was the journey of my second career, or maybe an evolution of my first. I am a constant learner and was on a mission to understand the most important thing in my life—me! This mission began with questions: *Who am I? Why am I here? And what is most important to me?*

These were huge concepts, ones that all humans wrestle with, and I knew answers wouldn't come overnight.

After weeks of introspection and exploration my Identity Statement evolved into:

I am the radiant sunlight on the ripples of transformation; my purpose is to transform how people see themselves as leaders and to be the leader they want to be and to mentor others to lead themselves. What is most important to me is to contribute in a meaningful way, have fun, be grateful, and continue learning and teaching.

Again, the hard reality bashed my brain: how do I translate that mission into a job?

At the time, I was transitioning away from a corporate pharmaceutical career. While I was good at my job and enjoyed what I did, I knew it was time for more fulfillment. To turn my vision into reality I tackled another series of questions. *What do I love to do? What do I like to do? And what am I capable of doing?*

Often people limit their career searches to what they are capable of. If I'd approached that transition that way, I would have simply gone to another pharmaceutical company or just stayed where I was. That possibility sparked no fire in my belly, and answering these tough questions helped me discover my love of teaching. I love to help people get promoted, guide others to be better leaders, and increase their ability to step up and shine.

Ah-ha! Executive coaching was the answer. Leveraging and leaning into my experience in corporate and my desire to teach, turned into a lucrative coaching business and teaching career. The lesson: challenge yourself, push beyond the easy answers, not only what are you capable of, but what you love to do. Let these answers guide your next steps and do not let fear stop you.

Today is my sixty-second birthday, eligible for some retirement benefits, and a lifetime National Parks pass! I want to travel and experience the world in an unencumbered way. As I sit on this beach, I reflect on the whirlwind of the last two years.

It started when I was going to live in Florida, on my cousin's sailboat for the winter. I was so excited and dreamt of the experience. Then came Hurricane Ian and with it went my floating home. Equally, if not more devastated than my cousin, I was crushed; and darkness threatened to take over. Not wanting to succumb to the sadness I challenged myself again: *How can I get the same experience without the boat? What is the experience I wanted?* I wanted freedom, travel, flexibility, a way to experience the world differently.

I bought a camper for my sixtieth birthday. The vision of traveling all over the country was so enthralling that I asked myself, why do I need a house? I could coach virtually and teach online from Alaska! Canada! And all the State and National Parks. Covid changed the world and made it not only acceptable, but even preferred, to engage and instruct remotely. The road was calling me. When I told friends and family, I was met with reactions from "It's a perfect idea," "How exciting!" "Are you crazy?" and even "You're going to be a Dateline episode!"

It has been nearly two years since, and I haven't stopped moving. I enjoyed Florida winters, explored loads of National and State Parks, enbibed at countless wineries and breweries, soaked in the culture at museums and roadside attractions. The largest ball of Twine is a sight to be seen, and Johnny Cash's boyhood home was nostalgic. I've camped on the Swanee River where I watched locals hunt for alligators, rafted 250 miles of the Grand Canyon, and participated in the Seattle Pride parade. The lesson: Regardless of what other people think is right for you, chase your happiness with wild abandon.

Try and align your life *In Flow*, you cannot find fulfillment when you wedge yourself into a life that is not meant for you. Things don't happen all at once; but with gathering momentum and a consistent willingness to heed your heart's calling you will find joyful contentment awaits.

Recently, a friend said "Retirement has three phases: The Go Phase; The Slow Go Phase, and the No Go Phase." I plan to stay in the Go Phase and keep the Slow and No-Go Phases at bay for as long as possible.

Recently, I stumbled along a little town called Seneca Falls. Who knew this was the site of the first women's rights convention, where over 300 men and women organized it in 1848. This convention began a seventy-two-year battle to gain the right for women to vote in the United States.

It's very humbling to think it took so long to bring about what we take for granted. The bravery of these women really sank in. Until this time, women were property, with no rights whatsoever. It made me reflect on how time has evolved for women in the workplace. I remember in the late eighties when my great boss called me Lawrence, because all good salespeople were men. I took it as a compliment; I didn't know anything else. In the nineties, I courageously asked why I didn't get the same bonus as my male colleague.

The answer was "he has a family to support" or when I questioned taking red eye flights all over the country, the response was "because he has kids." I didn't even think much of it when I was told to wear higher heels, shorter skirts and more lipstick. This was just common banter that you got used to and blew it off. Even as diversity, equity, and inclusion (DEI) became the corporate mantra, things really didn't change that much. True, diversity of gender and race improved but attitudes didn't. I wonder now if it ever truly will?

As I pondered this question, it came to me that I can still contribute (following one of my values). I recommitted myself to continue the quest these brave women started 177 years ago. Women deserve equity and recognition for their contributions and their worth. I've always loved coaching emerging women leaders and now I know this is the best way I can add value to the world. There is more work to do, and I know I am not done yet!

I encourage you, the reader, to remember "You are not done yet!" You have the ability and maybe the obligation to continue to add value. There is always more to experience, to mentor, to teach, and to live your best life. You've earned the right to live your passion, to be heard, and to contribute in ways that bring joy, equality, and enlightenment. We have work to do, and we are not done yet!

Lessons:

Identity: Who am I?

Purpose: Why am I here?

Values: What is most important to me?

Your passion:
- What do I love to do?
- What do I like to do?
- What am I capable of doing?

Retirement phases:
- The Go Phase
- The Slow Go Phase
- The No Go Phase

Do not let fear stop you.
Pay it forward.
Leverage your lessons.
Have fun.
You are not done yet.

INTRODUCTION TO
DIANNE BOYER

Dianne Boyer is a personal stylist helping professional women and women over 50 rediscover their confidence and joy through style. After decades in corporate and fashion marketing, Dianne transitioned into styling to empower women navigating life's next chapter. She offers practical, personalized styling for women who want to feel vibrant and relevant at any age.

Reinvention is not just about what she does for others, it's her own story as well. Her professional path includes leadership roles in Fortune 100 marketing and over a decade in the fashion accessories space. Since the beginning, her career has centered around brand identity, visual impact, and helping others make a strong first impression. She's leveraged her years of marketing experience and love of fashion and applied the same principles for making brands shine to doing the same for women.

Dianne has shared her styling insights on television segments in Detroit and Chicago and has been featured in *Real Simple*, *People*, and *Today.com*. Her message is simple:

it's never too late to reinvent yourself. Whether it's a career pivot or a fresh outfit, you deserve to love what you see in the mirror.

Joy in the Mirror

"Let's go get the mail," I say to Archie, and he dutifully wags his tail.

Every day, every time we get the mail, he gets excited. He loves being outside, even if it's just for a few minutes. But this day was different, because I was excited too! I was expecting something in the mail that took decades to arrive. I opened the mailbox and peered in and saw a small stack of envelopes.

"Sit," I told Archie, so that I could flip through the stack with both hands.

It was there!

I tore off the end of the envelope and pulled out the certificate.

I did it! I was a Personal Stylist!

My new adventure at sixty-three!

Five decades ago, I read my first fashion magazine and haven't stopped since. Life is like a winding road, and my journey took me through twenty years in corporate roles, then twelve at a small business, then three years as a fashion blogger, all before my dream of being a personal stylist came true.

I grew up in New Jersey with a mom who loved fashion. She dressed me in the cutest, most stylish gear. What I loved most was watching her get dressed, especially for parties and events, and I dreamt about being just like her. She wore a matching necklace and earring set for special events. It was an iridescent set of pearls that, when the light hit them just right, a kaleidoscope of colors danced across the gem. She was glamorous. She kept that set for her entire life, and now those pearls are mine. Each time I hold them, my awe returns and reminds me of our shared love of fashion.

When I was seven years old, my father's job relocated us to Athens, Greece, for a position at General Motors (GM). We spent over five years living there and traveling all over the continent. Mom understood the importance of my brother and me seeing the world and experiencing different cultures. We traveled throughout Europe and even visited Israel and the U.S.S.R. It was an incredible virtual classroom for a kid to learn how people are different yet the same. I was always dressed in a perfect travel outfit, thanks, of course, to my mom. An early deposit in the proverbial piggy bank for my future fashion career!

Living overseas helped me develop my personal style in a way you might not expect. I went to an American school, but there wasn't much access to American things. I wasn't as influenced by Western trends, and I didn't feel the need to be cool because it just wasn't an option. I picked my clothes and the looks I liked, and didn't feel pressured to wear what everyone else wore. But I was desperate for a Hang Ten t-shirt with the cute footprints, but never got one.

After our time in Greece, we returned to New Jersey just in time to start high school. After high school, we moved again—this time to Detroit, where I still live, in the heart of the automotive industry. Living in the Motor City and seeing everyone around me, both friends and family, working in the auto industry, ultimately influenced me and led me to my first job out of college. And even though I never really loved cars, I thought working in the industry was the place to be. Like my dad I went to work at General Motors.

My career aptitude tests in high school always included creative fields, such as graphic design, journalism, and marketing. In college, I considered all those fields and thought marketing looked interesting and it was an instant love! It played a role throughout my career. But it didn't start that way.

No marketing positions were available when I started my career, and I ended up supporting the business aspects of engineering, including hiring, budgets, and program management. It was a great training ground, and I still apply the skills I learned there today—I'm a spreadsheet ninja, even at sixty-three! But it didn't feed my creative side, after several years on the business side, I finally moved into the field I loved—marketing. I didn't know at the time how significant this opportunity was for me, both professionally and personally.

This opportunity took me to the Saturn division of

General Motors, whose marketing tagline was "A different kind of company, a different kind of car." Everything at Saturn was different: from the purchase experience to the driving experience, to the customer experience, where a specific kind of customer loyalty thrived.

My first assignment was being part of the management team for "The Saturn Homecoming," where 44,000 customers attended a uniquely special two-day appreciation event at the Saturn manufacturing complex in Spring Hill, Tennessee. Once we had the go-ahead, we had just six months to pull it off, and we did it!

It's hard to believe that 44,000 people visited where their car was born, but they did and they loved it. There were two football fields of activities for all the guests, including a concert stage. There were engineering displays, games for kids, food, and drink—you name it. We even had Wynonna Judd as the headliner for the evening concert. But the biggest draw was the plant tour.

Everyone who attended could not wait to see the cars on the assembly line. It brought joy not just to the attendees but also to the Saturn team members. In retrospect, it was the first event that made me realize you can both create joy and find joy in your work.

The event was a smashing success and widely celebrated in the industry. It earned prestigious awards, including "One of the Top 100 Marketing Success Stories of 1994" by *Advertising Age* and the "National Promotion of the Year" award from the Promotion Marketing Association of

America. Not a bad place to start. The Saturn Homecoming showed me what impactful marketing looked like and led to a wild fifteen years of success in my field.

Over those years, I worked on a wide variety of events. I spent most of my time at Chevrolet, focusing on sports and entertainment marketing. As a result, I worked on large, well-known events such as the Grammys, the Country Music Awards, the National Figure Skating Championships, the Olympics, and NASCAR. But my favorite opportunity was being an Olympic Torch Bearer.

I ran with the torch on its way to Salt Lake City for the 2002 Olympics, on a freezing January day in Akron, Ohio. But if I was cold on the outside, I was warm on the inside. To become an Olympic torchbearer, you had to be nominated by one of your peers at Chevrolet. Chevrolet had limited torchbearer spots as part of their sponsorship. Knowing that one of my fellow team members thought enough of me to submit my nomination made the entire experience much more meaningful.

I got to work on fashion-related events too. We partnered with Condé Nast magazines, Macy's, and the music and fashion event "Fashion Rocks." I managed a partnership between Rolling Stone magazine and the Hard Rock Café, showcasing Chevrolet's role in pop culture. However, I was also involved in smaller events such as the Future Farmers of America convention and the Car Enthusiast Clubs. I got to experience many different cities, people, and events that all left a lasting impression.

But one of the most important lessons at General Motors came as I leaned on the wooden boards of a chilly ice-skating rink. As part of the figure skating program at Chevrolet, I put together this event for young ice skaters. I watched as aspiring skaters twirled amongst their idols. Michelle Kwan and Todd Eldredge glided over the ice, and the boys and girls were in awe. They were on the same rink as Olympians. None of them could stop grinning, and their rosy cheeks reflected their starry eyes. My breath caught in my throat. Their joy was a gift from me. I did this.

I relish and hold onto the feeling I created for the young athletes to skate with their Olympic heroes. To the outside world, it wasn't the most visible or successful event I had worked on, but to me, it was the most meaningful. I brought happiness to people, and that solidified my sense of success. That's the day that I learned that it's not just about what we do, it's about how we make people feel.

These distinctive and powerful experiences taught me about people's uniqueness, interests, and how to connect with them where they are. One of the most valuable lessons I learned is that you must first understand what people are passionate about and who they are, and then you can address a need or satisfy a curiosity. Seeing people this way is an important skill not just for a stylist but in any capacity or application.

These experiences taught me about brand representation, the key to understanding the importance of "image." Attending these events taught me not just how important it is to represent your company, but also how to carry yourself. I represented my company on national television, to car dealers, customers, and more. How I looked and how I came across were important. I knew people formed opinions on the company and me based on my behavior. Since I already loved fashion, I worked hard to combine my love for fashion with marketing and built a personal brand. This combination is a key component of my current business as a stylist.

Then came my first big pivot. I met my husband, Jeff, who had lost his wife three years earlier and was a single dad to three boys, aged ten, fifteen, and seventeen. Because of the upheaval in their lives over the previous years, I decided to leave General Motors and focus all my attention and energy on my new family. My life changed quickly from a single career woman to a full-time mom of three boys.

This time was immersive and powerful, and it was time well spent. It was intimidating at first. I knew that I could never take the place of their mom, nor did I want to. Knowing how close I was to my mother, I tried to put that in perspective. I instead, I tried to create my relationship with each of them based on friendship and trust. If nothing else, I wanted them to know that they could always count on me. From simple things, like making school lunches, to conversations about "what makes girls tick," my goal was to be a support system for them. They are all excellent and successful men today with their own families. I did ok.

In retrospect, this period was significant for me

personally and professionally. I most likely would have stayed at General Motors for the rest of my career because I was comfortable there. At GM, I knew the work and the people, but I often ask myself, would I have grown if I had stayed?

After three years, I started to get the itch to return to work, but now I had a blank slate. I could do whatever I wanted, and I thought about what that might be. The only thing I knew for sure was that I didn't want to return to the automotive industry. It was time to try something different. But living in Detroit, it's not easy not to work on something not even loosely related to cars. I had to be patient; honestly, I didn't worry about it. I wasn't going to force-fit something to go back to work. I continued to enjoy my time with the boys while keeping my eyes and ears open for the right opportunity.

My opportunity appeared in a tiny ad in my hometown newspaper: marketing and public relations (PR) at a local handbag company, K. Carroll Accessories. It utilized my marketing skills and moved me closer to my first love of fashion. The job offered a flexible schedule, was a small business, and was only ten minutes from my house. I was still home for the boys, allowing me to continue using the professional skills I had worked hard to cultivate.

This move into fashion lit a new fire in me. I appointed myself the trends guru for the company and immersed myself in knowing what trends were essential and relevant to the business. I learned to navigate interests for a product with a six-month lead time and how to predict which items would still be relevant once production is complete. This close study honed my fashion skills and knowledge, and I was good at predicting the future desires of our customer base.

Coming from a Fortune Top Ten company with thousands of employees to a small business with fewer than ten employees was a significant change. There are pros and cons to each. Working at a large company with a large budget to match allowed me to do many things on a large scale. Working at a small business with a limited budget forced me to be more creative and innovative. It taught me that a small business doesn't mean you have to think small. Just the opposite is true. A small business is where you need to think big! There is nothing off-limits.

One day, I was watching Deals & Steals with Tory Johnson on Good Morning America (GMA), and I thought *We should be on that show.* Now, why would I believe that a small handbag company with ten employees from Detroit would make it on national television? Well, why not?

I dug through my contacts and sent tons of emails, getting mostly polite declines as a response. There was an event when Tory Johnson came to Detroit as part of a GMA promotion, and the owner of the company and I made sure to attend. We had the opportunity to talk with Tory about our handbags and to put a face to the name. I continued my quest, and after a year of concerted effort, K. Carroll Accessories debuted on Deals & Steals! That was

2016, and almost ten years later, they are still a regular part of that segment.

If GMA wasn't off limits, neither was my favorite soap opera, General Hospital! I watched the show regularly and noticed that the women carried handbags in almost every scene. *We should be on that show!* My research led me to the Head Costume Designer and the studio's mailing address. I boxed up a collection of handbags and sent them to him!

To my surprise, he called me the day they arrived to tell me he was thrilled. What I worried might be viewed as intrusive, he saw as an initiative that solved a problem. It turned out he was always trying to find handbags for each character every day, and I helped him solve this problem at no cost to the production company. And today, K. Carroll Accessories bags are still featured on the show.

All this makes me think: if I had never left General Motors, would I have ever really embraced the think big philosophy? It was in me all along, but with the restrictions and approvals required in corporate life, it was a concept that was hard to put into motion at a big company. Working at a small business taught me to dig deep, think about what I wanted, and just go for it.

While I was working on my think big philosophy for the small business, and while it was rewarding, I started thinking it was time to think big for myself. After twelve years of working there, and the entirety of my fifties, I felt I was approaching a now or never scenario for myself. It was time to put my philosophy into action, but this time for myself.

I have a sign on my desk at home that says, "There are only seven days in a week, and someday isn't one of them."

In 2016, my mother passed away at age eighty-five. While she had a long life, it's still hard to lose your mom, no matter how old you are. She died just a few weeks after the handbags from K. Carroll Accessories were on national television. I was happy that she got to see that accomplishment.

I continued working at K. Carroll, but in addition to the think big philosophy, I also felt that I wanted to do something that would honor my mom. The first thing that came to mind, and I missed most about her, was how we shared a love of fashion. We took a lot of trips together, including multiple trips to New York City, just to shop. Whatever I did next needed to be about fashion. It just had to be. Besides, now working in fashion marketing, I was halfway there.

One thing about my mom: she didn't just influence me about fashion, she also influenced my two nieces, my brother's daughters. My niece, Jen, and I started discussing different things we could do about fashion that would honor my mom. Together, we came up with The Harper Girls blog. My other niece, Brittany, lived four hours away; it was too hard to include her on a daily basis. Jen and I were the front women for the blog with support from Brittany behind the scenes.

We created a fashion and beauty blog focused on "How to Wear It at Any Age" because it represented my mom's identity. She was stylish every day of her life. She would get up every morning, take a shower, apply her makeup, and get fully dressed every single day. She never felt that she was too old to look good and that it was important to look and feel your best every day. That became a focus of "The Harper Girls."

It became a blog with a purpose. It was fun but also therapeutic. It allowed me to go back in time and think about all the things my mom had taught me about fashion and how they apply today. Like the age-old question: Can you wear white after Labor Day?

But it also became more for me. It also reinvigorated my love of fashion, especially clothing. I found myself spending hours researching fashion trends, window-shopping to see what was selling in stores, and immersing myself in all things style-related overall. Jen and I did this for over three years and were featured on local television and print magazines. We were able to have fun and share my mom's story. Mission accomplished.

Of course, as life goes, things change. Jen had her second child and needed to refocus on her family and career. Being a working mom of two toddlers kept her busy enough without the work that went into the blog (and there was a lot of it). That's when I started thinking about how to continue my love of fashion in a new way: solo! But I needed to figure out if I was ready and determine what I needed to know to take this new path.

Luckily for me, I have always loved learning. I was one of those kids who loved school. After college, I got my master's degree just to become better educated. While I gave a lot of thought to becoming a stylist, I also believed there was more I had to learn beyond my self-teaching. I found a great program that taught me much about styling and the styling business and provided official certification.

And now here we are. All my past experiences are aligning to create this perfect next chapter as a stylist. I find it interesting that we can't always see the alignment happening as we go through it. Experiences all feel like isolated chapters until we look back and see how they all worked together to shape our future.

For example, at General Motors, I learned how marketing to different groups and people gives you a better understanding of a client's needs and wants. It also taught me much about representing yourself in the corporate world, both as a brand and an individual.

At K. Carroll Accessories, I learned how to think big. How not to let what you think might be impossible limit your dreams.

As co-founder of The Harper Girls, I learned to combine what you love with what you do. And as a woman over fifty, I've learned that the only limits to what you can do are self-imposed.

That's the beauty of life experiences and how they frame the future. Sure, all my professional experiences gave me the knowledge, wisdom, and confidence to pivot my career more than once. But it's combining those practical experiences with the emotional ones that makes it sweet, and that's why I know I'm in the best place possible to share what I've learned with others.

There's a scene in the movie St. Elmo's Fire that has stayed with me since I first watched the movie forty years ago in 1985. Mare Winningham's character, Wendy, has just moved into her first apartment, and she's talking about making a peanut butter and jelly sandwich in the middle of the night. She says, "You want to know what's great? Last night I woke up in the middle of the night to make myself a peanut butter and jelly sandwich, and you know, it was *my* kitchen, it was *my* refrigerator, it was *my* apartment, and it was the best peanut butter and jelly sandwich that I have had in my entire life."

That's exactly how I felt when I started my own business. I picked the name of my company, Dianne In Style. I created the logo. I wrote the business plan. But the best part? I get to decide, every day, how I can help other women. It's my version of the peanut butter and jelly sandwich.

Seeing that in action was a surreal moment for me. For my first television segment on over 50 style for WGN-TV in Chicago, they showed my company's name and logo on the screen at the end of the segment. It was the proof point that my career had come full circle. From being one of thousands of employees at a large corporation to seeing the business name I created on a television screen decades later feels more than just an accomplishment. It's pure joy.

But it's even more than that. Being a stylist today allows me to give a different kind of gift to professional women and women over fifty. I empower them to rediscover their confidence through fashion. Motivated by the belief that style has no age limit, I want to help women build wardrobes that make them joyful and confident.

I love working with clients who see what they wear as more than just clothes, but rather an extension of their personal brand. From revisiting their wardrobe to better align with their company's branding, to creating looks for a Board of Directors position, I love finding ways to blend a client's personal style with their business goals.

In addition to working with clients, sharing my fashion knowledge is essential to me. Television segments and contributing to style articles on Real Simple, People, and today.com are not just a way to share knowledge but also to continue learning and staying current. My work for these segments and articles also benefits my clients, as I pass along what I've learned in our styling sessions. It's another way to keep moving forward.

While most days I'm a stylist, some days I'm just a girl who misses her mom. She would have loved everything I'm doing today, and I know she would have been proud. If she were here, she would laugh at the idea that she's been the inspiration behind all of it. But the truth is, what started as an homage to her evolved into a full-blown career pivot. She would never have believed that making sure I had a travel outfit for vacations and the hours spent shopping at the mall for back-to-school clothes would have such a lasting impact. Thanks, Mom!

I am positioned to do what I love every day. Instead of reading fashion magazines for fun, I read them for knowledge. I study trends and go shopping to see what stores are selling. But that's not where the joy in being a stylist comes from. The satisfaction comes from helping others feel good and confident in what they wear and how they present themselves. I firmly believe everyone's path has a purpose and should be shared when and where it can help others the most.

Some journeys are straight lines, clearly defined with a purpose, a plan, and a destination. Some take winding roads. You may not see what's around the corner, but you keep driving. And then there are lives like mine, which seem like a series of off-ramps and on-ramps. When you find joy at the end of the road, you'll know you were on the right path all along.

INTRODUCTION TO
JANET WINKLER

Janet is the Co-Founder of The Difference Lab, born out of her desire to solve a pressing issue: we all have too much to do and not enough time to do it. We're cramming more in, doing more, with a creeping sense that busywork is overtaking essential work in our professional lives, and that we're not doing what really matters in our personal ones.

Enter intentional subtraction: the wildly underused strategy of fiercely focusing on what drives value by subtracting what doesn't. It's *simplify to amplify*.

The Difference Lab has helped individuals, teams and leaders across the globe shift from busywork to essential work. From checking the boxes to creating impact. We call it "Impact by Design"—a deliberate move away from activity to outcomes, with intentional subtraction at its core. We imagine the end of a workday where you close your laptop and think, *"Damn, I really crushed it today."*

Janet is an accomplished business leader, senior executive, and entrepreneur. Her career began at Procter & Gamble in Brand Management, followed by founding

In-sync (doing business as [dba] in-sync), an insights-based brand consultancy for global consumer and healthcare clients. After In-sync was acquired by Publicis Groupe, she served as Group President at Publicis Health and Chief Strategy Officer. Janet then joined McKinsey & Company as a Senior Advisor. But, at her core, she's a creator—and The Difference Lab was calling.

Janet is a proud mother to three adult children, trying real hard every day to be a good mother-in-law to their three partners (it's a work-in-progress), and working to be the kind of fun, fit, ready-for-anything grandmother her three grandsons and dog Frankie deserve.

Forget Grit. My Power Move Was Subtraction by Design.

INTRO: THE MYTH THAT KEEPS ON GIVING

If I were a Girl Scout, my sash would be decorated with so many badges, my five-foot-four frame would struggle to stay upright under the weight of all that hard-earned glory.

Let's be clear—it's not for hiking, camping or sewing, but for resilience, perseverance, grit, and endurance. Except I was never a Girl Scout.

I quit Brownies at seven because they made us dance around a paper mâché mushroom. While I loved the uniform, and I still love a uniform-on others, and admired the badges, I knew it wasn't for me. The mushroom thing was somehow just too much. Apologies to former Brownies and Girl Scouts: I respect your path. I had my own.

I'm the third of three kids, which means I was born negotiating for attention and figuring things out on my own. I had to ride shotgun, adapt, and find my way without a map. I was both shy and bold—an odd combo, but it worked. That's the first badge I earned: Make your own rules.

Fast forward to adult life, and those Girl-Scout qualities—grit, hustle, hang-in-there energy are everywhere. We celebrate them. Revere them. We're told they're the bedrock of success.

And we learn them early.

Remember, *The Little Engine That Could?* That chipper little train, against all odds, hauling a massive load up a mountain? Sure, it's about believing in yourself—"I think I can, I think I can"—let's call it for what it is: that pipsqueak of a train made it up the mountain through sheer grit, determination and refusing to give up.

Maybe it started there for me, too. But the moment this concept really landed was "meeting" Rocky Balboa. The underdog. The two-bit boxer. The raw-egg-gulping, frozen cow carcass punching, sweat-fueled lunatic who sprinted up the steps of the Philadelphia Museum like his life depended on it.

I've done none of that.

I was a teenager when *Rocky* hit the screen. I too was determined to make my mark. Like Rocky, my rise would take grit, relentlessness and a fair bit of pain.

The hustle and hang-in-there message was the drumbeat of the business world.

"Grit" became a buzzword, a hiring filter, and a leadership predictor.

Candidates who "hung in there" when the going got tough, who didn't walk away, were seen as leadership material.

Here's the reveal:

Yes.

But also no.

Because if I had hung in there and made it work at every step, my career would have been successful, but fine. But it wouldn't be the exhilarating, risk-taking, boundary-breaking, build something from scratch career that I get to say was mine.

Just because you can make something work doesn't mean you *should*.

ACT 1: THE GOLDEN LADDER— HANG IN THERE: YOU GOT GRIT

Right out of university, I scored the golden ticket of marketing: Brand Management at Procter and Gamble. Marketers called it the Ivy League MBA in marketing. It promised world-class training in general management, marketing, and leadership. It delivered.

P&G and I weren't exactly a match made in career heaven.

I'm a color-outside-of-the-lines, don't-salute-the-title, let's-just-get-it-done sort of woman. They were a slow-moving, prove-it-before-you-do-it, proudly hierarchical, well-oiled machine kind of place.

Despite our character differences, I loved it—for a while. The people were super smart. The rigor was unmatched. P&G had world-class data and best practices to learn from.

I worked on big launches—catnip for someone like me who thrives on building from scratch, ambiguity, and rapid problem solving. It wasn't the rinse and repeat of the classic brand. Orange juice was one. It tanked. Liquid Tide was another (it crushed). I was learning like crazy, running hard, and I loved the unpredictably. I was all in.

Until I wasn't.

Then came Mike. My fast-paced adventure screeched to a halt. I was excited to report to Mike—he was two levels up—who led the whole division from marketing to the factories, from sales to finance. He was experienced, smart, and kind. He was a micromanager of Olympic caliber.

He loved marketing a little too much. He dove in the weeds, revisited decisions, and turned tasks into slow-motion loops. What had been fast-paced and exciting became a slog of déjà vu.

But I was Rocky! Right? I had grit. Pay your dues. Stick it out, Janet.

So I did. For months. I was frustrated and drained. I was wasting time and talent. The spring in my step? Gone.

Then came the moment. The one that changed everything.

One morning while brushing my teeth and venting again to my husband, Howard, he said the thing that changed everything:

"Quit."

Foam and fury were spilling from my mouth.

"What did you just say?"

"Just quit," he repeated. Dead serious.

My first thought: When was the last time he quit? What

did he know about anything? He's a lawyer.

His emotional ultimatum was the jolt that I needed. Who was this woman in a blue suit, nylons, and low-heeled pumps?

Wake up and welcome back, friend. That woman in the mirror was the high school student who started a pool-cleaning business at sixteen. The university student who was nearly arrested for throwing a pie in the face of a small-town politician. Because of another business I started: The Hired Gun. We did anything legal that someone paid us to do. I was the person who was least likely to work at a place like P&G.

Could I quit?

Hell yes.

I stopped waiting for the situation to change. I stopped looking to prove that I would hang in there and somehow make it work.

Three months later, I launched my own market research business, blending branding expertise with deep insight work.

And just like that, In-sync was born.

That chapter thrilled me more than any other in my career. We built something powerful. We were pioneers in using new ways to decode human behavior. We developed repeatable methodologies and systems to enable scalability and increase profitability. In-sync grew to over one-hundred employees, worked on multi-billion dollar brands, gained global recognition, and created a culture where the smartest most creative people I would ever work with thrived.

The lesson? Yes, grit is valuable. But it can trap you. This need to strive and persevere must be balanced with knowing when to quit, walk-away, or change. Grit only matters if it's taking you somewhere you actually want to go.

ACT 2: THE MOTHERHOOD ILLUSION—
HANG IN THERE. CRAM MORE IN.

Three years into In-sync, I had my first of three kids. Two more followed in the next four years. It was beautiful. And brutal.

I was a founder, leader and doer, and a mother of three under five years old.

The "cram in all in years" era began. Already on the hamster wheel of life, my little legs started pumping faster. I juggled a growing business, global travel, motherhood, household management, holidays, after-school activities, and the endless scheduling of everything. And the mental load of "what will emotionally scar my children if I miss it?"

I had to "create memories" raise responsible, ethical humans, and be a good partner to Howard—who was in it with me all the way.

I believed good moms maintained high standards on everything. I crammed more in. I didn't drop the ball. I ran faster. Juggled more. I hung in there.

Rocky had nothing on me.

I believed the lie: it *will* get easier. When they're out of diapers. When they're in school. When they do homework on their own.

Then the biggest lie of all—it will be easier when they're teenagers.

Spoiler: It never got easier. The pain points were just different.

Cramming more in isn't a strategy. It's a slow burn to exhaustion.

I dug deep. I hung on and had Lion King moments.

We splurged on Lion King Broadway Theater tickets. I raced home from work. The kids? Not ready. Not even close. Worse, they wanted to keep playing rather than get ready for a special night. We were $500 deep, and they couldn't be bothered.

What a bunch of ungrateful, too privileged, rotten kids. Shouldn't they be waiting excitedly—hair brushed, in party clothes and bursting with gratitude?

I lost it.

Completely.

Full throttle meltdown.

Panic, urgency, yelling, crying—mine and theirs.

I tried to enjoy the show, but the freak-out left its mark.

Times like those made it painfully clear: I couldn't wait for things to get better.

I had to design my life better.

I did:

- I quit driving carpool. It wasn't bonding. It was road rage with seatbelts.

- I opted out of bake sales, hot dog days, and playground duty.

Instead, I picked high-impact moments to invest in:

- One class trip per kid per year.
- One-on-one Starbucks hot chocolate dates.
- Family weekends not jam-packed itineraries.

I hired an executive assistant at work—lifesaving. Maybe I could have used the money for greater business impact, but this was an invaluable investment. My life, my family, my sanity demanded it.

The lesson? Stop waiting for the "it will get better" fairy to rescue you. Design your life with intention. Ruthlessly focus on what matters. Courageously drop the rest.

ACT 3: SELLING MY COMPANY—
HANG IN THERE. "YOU'RE NOT WORTH ENOUGH."

By the time I hit fifty, I knew I wanted to sell In-sync.

We had built something smart, profitable, and world-class.

Not just a business. A culture. A brain trust. A brand I was proud of.

But selling? That's next level scary. What if no one wanted us? What would happen to the team I had poured my heart into?

I had no clue what I was doing. Still, I was ready.

We started the process: Getting a valuation—how much did the "outside world" estimate our business was worth? A valuation is a financial term and a process that establishes the market value of a company or an asset. We met with two respected firms—the kind that are supposed to know what the market will pay, how to best position you, and who might bite.

The first firm came back with a number. It was surprisingly low and depressing.

Low enough to make me question if we had anything valuable to sell.

They were experts. Confident in their math. The senior guy spoke slowly, wisely, and confidently.

They said our business wouldn't be highly valued. Finding a buyer would be difficult. We need to drive more revenue, expand our client base, reduce costs. Hang in there. Keep grinding. Wait for a better time.

I almost believed them. Almost.

Because the truth is, when other people doubt your worth—especially when they have spreadsheets and concise speech to prove it—it's easy to accept it.

It poked at every fragile part of my confidence. Every quiet "we're just a..." and "I'm just a..." started screaming in my head. But fortunately, we had set meetings with two firms.

The second firm got it. They listened to our story, to our passion, to me and my partners. They saw the brand strength, the impressive client list, the repeatable systems, the culture you couldn't fake. They wanted us to succeed. They believed in our worth. And that belief mattered.

Their valuation? Significantly higher than the first firm. We chose them.

We received multiple offers. We chose the buyer who was the best fit and who we felt was the right partner for our company and our culture.

In-sync was acquired.

The trap? When others underestimate you, it's easy to start shrinking yourself to fit their spreadsheet or their perception of your value. I almost did.

The lesson? Don't wait for others to declare your worth. Know it yourself. Act on it.

ACT 4: THE BIGGEST AHA! THE MYTH-BUSTING FINALE

This act? I didn't see it coming. I am a kid from a small city.

I am the daughter of super smart parents who never stepped foot in a corporate office. Never wore a lanyard. My dad owned a small lady's wear business. My mom who, like my dad, had only graduated high school, went to university in her forties. She crushed it.

Dad's business was successful, and enough to satisfy two goals that were out of reach for him as a child of immigrant parents: send his kids to overnight camp and put his kids through university. Done.

After selling In-sync my life was different. This kid from good, but still modest means, travelled the world for clients and sat in the front of the plane. The shy kid now commanded the stage and launched leaders.

I returned to corporate life, determined to do so on my own terms. I spent four years as Group President at Publicis Health living in New York. Then a year with McKinsey and Company as a Senior Advisor. Big titles. Big rooms. Big learning. But something bigger was bothering me.

Work had changed. And not for the better. People were pinged 24/7. Sprinting in urgency. Back-to-back meetings defined people's days. People were spent. Buried in motion—robbed of real impact. Thinking time was non-existent.

We were so flooded with our to-do list we were missing the good stuff—the wow work that bruises your brain, fires your intellect, and accelerates your growth. It wasn't just happening at the top. It was everywhere.

It hit me: What made my career wasn't grinding through all that wasted time and energy:

- At P&G I subtracted the boss, the structure, the path that no longer served me. But I waited too long.
- At home I subtracted obligations that drained me. But I crammed too long.
- When selling In-sync I subtracted others' assessment of my worth. But I doubted too long.

It wasn't endurance that got me here. It was intentional subtraction.

That's what fueled the creation of The Difference Lab— my next chapter and my boldest yet.

The Difference Lab is a business built on a simple belief:

We don't need to *add* more to succeed. We need to subtract what no longer serves.

At work, that means clearing clutter, reclaiming focus, and unleashing your wow work—the kind that demands your sharpest thinking, stretches your superpowers, and makes you say, *"I crushed it."* It requires us to spot the hidden friction—the invisible norms, habits, and expectations—that have crept into our ways of work, quietly fueling the overload.

In life, it means designing with intention. Choosing meaning over motion. Showing up for what matters—and dropping the rest.

The truth is: Work and life haven't just collided—they've detonated. The expectations are relentless. The busyness is glorified. And "hanging in there," grinding through, persevering just keeps you in the trap.

If you're stuck, don't ask what to add. Ask what to remove.

If you're leading a team, a company, or just trying to lead yourself—stop shoving more in. Start subtracting. With intention.

My Girl Scout sash could have been filled with badges.

Now I know: The most important move isn't adding, it isn't gritting through it. It's knowing what to subtract.

Know what badges to retire and to sew your sash with the most important few.

INTRODUCTION TO
CYNDY WULFSBERG

Cyndy Wulfsberg was born in Texas and has lived in six states, one territory, and two foreign countries. Early travels with her Air Force family inspired a lifelong interest in languages and cultures. She continues to study languages and travels extensively. Physical challenges led to a love of dance and commitment to whole body wellness. She is a proud Iyengar Yoga student and gym rat when she is home. She holds a BA from Luther College in Political Science, and an MA in Sociology from the University of Virginia. While writing throughout her life for entertainment, perspective and sanity she held traditional jobs in education, counseling, elected public office, consulting, negotiations and conflict resolution, lobbying, and national and international marketing and sales. She has served as executor for four family members and knows that hard things are easier with a dose of humor. Her recent bestselling book, *Ghost or Guardian, A Guidebook for the Pre-Dead, Do these things before you die so your heirs won't hate you later*, is a gentle nudge to complete your post life planning. As a reader she enjoys humor, science fiction, historical fiction, mysteries, and authors from around the world. As an author and speaker, she delves into her file cabinet to tap the trove of inspiration and experience she accumulated throughout her life before she pursued publication. She is devoted to her family and friends and lives in Michigan with her husband, cats and bees.

Do You Want to Tell a Story?

Most of us have at least a few books in us. We have stories to tell that may or may not be the ones we repeat to family and friends. We have trials we have suffered, paths not taken, misunderstood successes, and unacknowledged failures. We dreamt of things judged by ourselves or others as impractical or out of reach. And our careers may not be what we planned or aspired to, but what happened to us, with or without objection or enthusiastic consent.

Me too.

As a traveler through life I am often distracted by opportunities I did not expect, averse to closing doors that are long left propped open, unable to see paths that are open to me but unfamiliar and not captivating enough to become an irresistible calling. What I wanted I was afraid to want and doubted my ability to accomplish. My journey was destined to be indirect and messy, but ultimately amazing and fulfilling. And I still have prospects and discovery ahead. I compiled content before developing my craft by taking this route and both are essential to my success as an author, and the treasure in my file cabinet could not have been amassed with a more direct route.

I introduce myself to you as an author now, three years from my corporate retirement and one year from climbing out of my file cabinet with one of my many manuscripts, having published a best-selling book in print with a companion workbook and audiobook. And more to come!

I have an energizing purpose that was underdeveloped in my youth, impeded as an employee in the corporate world, and barely struggled to survive through personal and professional challenges. I am building and embracing an expanding network of enthusiastic and empowering colleagues and friends. I still have a somewhat bemused and curious network from my earlier life who never knew about my private habit of writing. My writing was always completely private throughout my time in school and traditional employment, and I worked through difficult or frustrating situations by writing about them.

I even killed off terminally annoying folks and tossed their discarded carcasses into my file cabinet, dispatched with my pen and keyboard. The idea that those needles in my side are transforming into inspiration and creative production today is a source of profound satisfaction and may offer a vision of forward thinking for others.

It is fair to wonder how I find myself where I am now, happily rummaging through my file cabinet of corpses, tales of vengeance, and problems analyzed in multiple ways, and why now and not earlier in my life? My journey is shaped by my life experience and influences and has been one of dodging and feinting progress resulting in a meandering path with no guiding direction or acknowledged goal other than a commitment that I would make the best of every opportunity and give it maximum effort. I was always moving, but not necessarily forward. I took Winston Churchill's definition of success to heart, "Success is stumbling from failure to failure without losing enthusiasm." But I didn't really believe I could succeed in my private dreams.

Let me explain.

I always wanted to be a successful published author, from my first adolescent diary throughout decades working in various pursuits. As a child the one request that was always granted was a request for a book. Books had power in my family relationships and in their ability to transform and expand our minds. The idea that I could have a piece of that power was compelling for a kid with chores and rules and expectations to meet. Success in school was highly valued, and my mother was the first in her family to go to college.

She was not supported in this goal by her parents who were not educated past high school, never owned their own home, and struggled with their smart and willful daughter. My father came from an educated family where an undergraduate degree was a minimum expectation. He was the baby of eleven children and several of his older siblings had advanced degrees in mathematics, music and physics. He began paying for his university education playing the bassoon in the Texas Symphony Orchestra. The degree was the important thing, not a musical career. As children of the Depression and wars growing up before social safety nets, the ability to make a living under any conditions was paramount. Arts and creativity might make your life worth living, but making a living was the priority.

Our families are the first social groups we navigate and find our place within, and this is not a group we easily dismiss since we are taught directly and indirectly and controlled intensely for many years. Our familial relationships are formative in complex ways we don't readily understand as we experience them, and our roles within the family group are shaped by pressures and circumstances that continually evolve.

I am a product of those metamorphic pressures, as are we all, but the perspective of time can provide insight. My parents were endlessly supportive and confident in my abilities to do anything despite my insecurities and trusted I would eventually figure it all out and find my own way as they had. My older brother was a challenge and a mentor to me and was willful and single minded where I was flighty and insecure. I wanted his approval as much as that of my parents. He was a musical savant, enjoying his art as a calming respite from his academic focus, while I sweated through piano competitions.

I was wait-listed at one Ivy after another, but he only applied to MIT having decided to attend when he was twelve years old. As a toddler he walked by his first birthday, and I did not walk until I was two. I was extremely flexible, and my pediatrician suggested I train to become a contortionist with the circus or try ballet to build up my strength.

From my early childhood of self-doubt, I forged ahead buoyed by the confidence of my parents and I adopted their belief that knowledge and education were "the keys to the kingdom." I energetically pursued success in school and ballet, but succeeding in school compared to my brother's genius and my parents swagger did not translate into growth of confidence for me. I cared about approval a lot and I used any perceived lack of it to alter my course. My parents were my role models for my aspirations, and I did not risk coloring outside the lines that I saw brought them happiness and success. In my family hard work and self-sufficiency were the characteristics that mattered.

My childhood flexibility issues developed into a love of ballet and success as a dancer. Dancing opened doors for me in school drama productions and in a ballet company and I worked hard at it as if I was pulling myself up to my two-year-old feet over and over again. In high school I was already dancing accompanied by the National Symphony Orchestra at venues that were thrilling and intoxicating. There were discussions with my mentors about where I should audition and opportunities for a professional career.

What happened next was a door closed and the beginning of deliberate neglect and tamping down of my creative soul. I was offered a scholarship in dance at a major university, but I subconsciously adopted the values of my parents, and I could not envision a life in dance and a concurrent academic or business oriented life. The fact that my parents never questioned my rejection of a full scholarship to face a future of helping me pay for college, solidified my belief that my decision was correct. I mourned the death of a mind-body discipline I knew I would never again achieve. I remember sobbing for hours without really knowing why. My decision was considered and reasonable. My tears were not.

I trampled my artistic aspirations and desires to march along the expected path to career success and maturity. I lost sight of a dream of my own and my confidence took a beating along with my creative nature. I went to college and worked on filling a toolbox of marketable skills through hard work, accomplishments, and certifications; and desperately hoped to please myself and others, without having a destination of my own in my sights or the confidence to look for a dream of my own.

What held me back from work that I wanted to do both in ballet and writing? Partly it was a lack of self-confidence and partly it was a question of the legitimacy of my dreams. I believed my limited world experience meant I had little to say that might interest or be valued by others. And I was not convinced I could make a living in dance. Despite succeeding in many areas, when I met a closed door or skeptical audience, I habitually trusted the judgement of others above my own and swerved away from the apparent roadblock. The weight of my insecurities impeded my progress more than the rejections of others.

In my youth, I wrote about what most teenagers write about; crushes, frustrations with friendships and family, and a determination to avoid decisions that would lead to regret. I was fencing myself in, even as I traveled toward adulthood. I dramatically burned most of this writing in the name of privacy and growing up and moving on. The ashes were testimony to my decision about the end of an era.

I studied Sociology in graduate school. I was drawn to the goal of observing human behavior and studying it analytically. I played at being grown up and looked for role models I could emulate. I attended a cocktail party to welcome Margaret Mead, the famous anthropologist, to our university. I worried over what to wear and what I might discuss with her.

The party was held in a grand colonial house unlike any place I had ever been. At first glance it was clear that Dr. Mead was probably more uncomfortable than I was. She accepted the circulating grad students as a trial she endured and limited her interaction to handshakes and nods. I took my turn, shaking her hand and fawning about her latest publication, wanting to stand out from the group as a rare woman in her field, but nothing profound came out of my mouth.

What is a stupid question when meeting Margaret Mead? Likely, all of mine. This was why I gave up dance!? To be a serious person! For what?! As prolific as she was as a researcher and writer, she did not hold the floor at the event. She was nervous and inarticulate, and I left disappointed in her and in myself. Ironically, she wrote extensively about children in primitive societies who repeated almost exactly the lives of their parents. What did that mean for me?

I struggled to find a research topic. My life experience was predominantly as a student, and I carved out an area of study in the education of medical doctors since my new husband was in medical school and I had a front row seat to his experience. It turns out that most entering medical students did not go into the field because they had great interpersonal and communication skills.

The medical curriculum of the time was designed to weed out those who could not stoically approach their patients as cases rather than people with fears and feelings. If the medical students weren't that good at turning off their empathetic side, maybe alcohol would help, and plenty of it was abused, setting up additional personal problems for those we depend on to save our lives in an emergency and nurture our wellness in health.

Medical students as a group had high levels of success in science and math, more than average left-handedness, discomfort with literature and languages, and were pushed to absorb facts above all and seek out every medical opportunity above human relationships. There was one disparaged class, in medical ethics, where the students took turns recording the class while most of them skipped it.

At the time, my study was groundbreaking. The common sense of tomorrow proposed, studied and validated by a small, easily overlooked woman in an academic department where I was not expected to excel. My thesis analyzed the medical school curriculum as preparation to interact with patients, specifically patients being stressed, ill or broken, in an intimidating environment and subjected to unfamiliar language and terms. Courses in communication and listening skills and even psychology were disparaged by the medical students as was any course work that was not thoroughly devoted to the fact base of medicine.

People only ended up in psychology if they couldn't stand the messiness of "real" medicine. Their future depended on being able to learn and retain facts of medicine, and they were quick to tell me I would want that too, if I were the patient in front of them. I am pretty sure no one at the medical school noticed or read my thesis, and I was not the salesperson I became later in life; and I did not attempt reform or publicity based on my analysis and results.

While navigating graduate school I collected part time jobs, thrilled that I could support myself and pay for my degree with my teaching assistant (TA) position at the university, work as a dance instructor, and sex educator and counselor for the local public school system. The local school system did not want any teacher on staff discussing anything about sex with students, so they outsourced sex ed to the local health department and staffed a phone answering center to handle concerns of teens. The best part of the job was helping teens with upset parents and teaching as a guest teacher where all the students definitely paid attention! The worst part of the job were all the uncomfortable remarks from the medical students I knew. My qualifications? Energy and a willingness to figure out how to do the jobs and accept low pay. I knew I could learn new things in very disparate areas and took satisfaction in accumulating skills and opportunities that primarily served my employers. I was focused on being in demand and filling my toolbox, eclectic as it was. The fact that people kept offering me jobs was satisfying and reinforced my value as a person able to make a living.

Eventually I took a position as a grant writer in the medical school which led to work as a research analyst designing computer-based health information systems, writing training manuals and training the staff. This felt like the most grown-up job of all and solidified my steps away from my artistic nature and into the adult and consequential world of work.

I wrote about frustrations with superiors in my jobs and school and started to write with humor for the first time, slanting frustrating events in ways that made my tormentors look foolish. There were characters galore, that were farcical caricatures I didn't even have to imagine but just needed to describe, and it was freeing to do it without fear of consequences. Maybe as a serious grownup I could be frivolous and a little mischievous in the dark of night with a pen in hand. I stopped burning my writing and my file cabinet was born.

This was my last employment period before a time of personal travel for my husband's work and family demands. My toolbox grew heavier, and my skill set expanded with logistical tasks, even as relationship growth was made more difficult by travel and distances involved. A gap in your resume is not something a career focused woman is excited about, even if I was able to indulge my writing habit more without the need to punch a clock for an employer. I needed the writing more than ever, faced with uncertainty about my future. My self-confidence waned without superiors feeding it, even if they were feeding it to support their goals instead of mine.

Writing about our travels and cultural observations became important to me, and I wrote about our children and growing family. I was still a Sociologist in my own mind, still subscribing to the journals I rarely read, but writing with some distance as an observer on some days, and as a hapless participant on others.

Eventually we moved back to mainland USA, and I began navigating public education on behalf of our children. The more I learned about public schools the more I wanted to be involved in improving them, and it was an area where women were active and occasionally in charge. I was involved in founding a public school watchdog organization and I edited a newsletter reporting on school board meetings which eventually resulted in a fourteen-year tenure on the Board of Education, thirteen of them as President.

I was active with the state organization supporting boards of education and a new state lobbying group advocating for districts with similar needs. The next step was a consulting business to help effectiveness and interpersonal relations within boards of education. Social problems and conflict resolution became my area of expertise. I began to teach at local universities. I was making a difference and began to see a path for my post-school-board career.

My meandering, opportunistic ways were working for me. My career track was developing and my creative outlet was my children whom I wrote for and about constantly. I was frustrated that there was no obvious path to publishing which I began to think of as a possible benefit and entertainment for others, even as I relied on my writing more heavily as a major tool of reflection and enjoyment for myself. These were the years where I committed the most murders in the dark of night with my pen. And if I didn't kill my tormentors, I made them suffer on the page. As bizarre as this sounds, it helped me maintain a well-controlled and widely acknowledged demeanor of calm and helped me become a better listener. I did not take my challenges with my work personally at all, and every conflict was new material.

Then there was a fork in the road. A move required for my husband's professional advancement and personal health and sanity meant a major upheaval for me and brutal severance from my developed network and opportunity. On the brink of a traditional career to which I aspired, with advancement, security, impact, and recognition, it was my turn to take one for the team. We moved to rural Iowa and bought a farm complete with cows, prairies, bluffs, historic house, few local friends, and my husband in the professional situation of his dreams, although with a notoriety he struggled to shoulder. I may as well have been flung out of a spaceship alone with no life support.

This was the perfect time for me to look at my writing and find purpose for it or burn it again, but this time to keep warm in the sub-zero temperatures. The move stimulated more writing as I dealt with culture shock and personal upheaval. I was antsy and distracted. I traveled frequently due to loneliness and difficulties with our house sale back east in a season of major economic recession.

When I was home in Iowa there were demands on my time and interruptions I didn't anticipate. I was not prepared to order truckloads of gravel for our quarter mile driveway before the ice set in. There were no adequate earplugs when calves were weaned, and cows mooed constantly. I learned how to effectively herd the cows that escaped our fences. If they make it to the road and cause a traffic accident it is potentially deadly and does homeowner's insurance cover that? Or what needs to happen when the barn blew down in our own personal extreme weather event? Or when the stone basement mortared with cream and sand happened to flood? Or when the wind picked up while we were dutifully burning the prairies to preserve them?

The house was heated with an oil furnace, propane heated water, and a wood stove, and I came to be grateful for the redundancy, if annoyed by the need to monitor supplies for all of it. There were coyotes everywhere and even an infamous traveling cougar on my porch! I didn't gather adequate tools in my previous life to be a good steward of the land or my home, or a good neighbor to those around me who were all at least a mile away and out of sight.

My husband suffered a sudden health crisis that focused my attention like nothing ever had. He could not work for months while recovering and it was unclear if he would be able to work again. This, after recently moving away from everyone I knew well who would have helped us. There was so much uncertainty and shock and pain, and I struggled to stop running from my situation.

Eventually I managed to stare our changed circumstances in the face and take inventory of my skills and tools at hand. I began to analyze our new reality and chose to deal with it. Or at least take steps to action and hope it fooled more people than just me. I learned about our new environs, investigated work and career opportunities for our support, and quit mewling about the writing in the file cabinet that called to me like a siren in a storm.

The result was my most unforeseen career move, but I took what was available and made the most of it, grateful for a job. I began a career in marketing veterinary products for dairy animals and support for research and chemical analysis for their health and management. The skills and knowledge required for this work were new to me, but I took on new things before, and knew I was trainable. Kind people who needed a reliable employee took the risk that a city person who cared and worked hard would turn out alright. The work eventually took me all over the country and abroad, and it became a service calling and crash course in how the world is fed, starting from the cows dropping calves in icy puddles outside my own front door, and ending up conveniently with food on grocery shelves and our dinner plates.

The work was enlightening beyond measure and transformed me into an ambassador from the farmland to the cities, able to recognize urban myths about the rural world that I previously believed in my ignorance and arrogance born of my ill-informed suburban point of view. Urbanites tend to believe that farmers aren't very bright, and don't understand prevailing concerns about food safety, ecology, and animal welfare. What I learned firsthand is that animal husbandry, crop farming and responsible care of the land and resources are essential to farmers' success and require highly technical skills, sophisticated education, and long-term commitment to a high-risk livelihood.

I may not have to use chemistry and math in my daily life, but those responsible for feeding the world need to use those disciplines daily. And they have to be committed and able to do hard physical work, manage daunting financial risk, forever changing governmental programs, oversight, and support, not to mention the weather and climate. I will step off my soap box for now, but if you struggle to keep your roses blooming, your yard green, and your patio tomato producing, imagine that the future of your children depends on your success managing those things over hundreds of acres and with serious financial investment in facilities and living resources.

As busy as I was, my writing bloomed in this environment

of novelty and exposure to new knowledge and people from different backgrounds. I was the oddball in my Midwest farming community and was repeatedly the obvious funny actor in my stories. I grew to love the character part as much as the cast of people generously supporting me.

The value of small-town USA was brought home to me repeatedly. When you are not buried in anonymous masses you barely acknowledge, you get to know and depend on your neighbors, colleagues and even strangers you meet. I could not pull over to take a photograph in the winter without the next car stopping to ask if I was ok. I met artisans and craftsmen and designed furniture with my Amish neighbors. I didn't refer to an app to find what I needed, I asked a person who thoughtfully responded to my needs. I took products to farmers who called with concerns about their cows and toured the best working dairy farms in the country as well as struggling ones. I really did get pretty good at herding cows.

My writing burgeoned in the file cabinet. I learned new skills and acquired tools that I didn't know existed. I learned the rhythms of the land and watched more sunrises in a few years than I saw in my previous lifetime. I felt like a part of the natural world rather than a suited up occasional observer of it. I started keeping bees and participated in local agriculture. My bees were subject to extreme weather and my inexperienced care. Some years we could have bathed in honey and other times I grieved to see thousands of dead bees on the snow, unable to make it back to their hive during a cold snap.

Academic Sociology taught me to value observation, but there is nothing like participation to focus where one looks. I was learning the questions to ask, both about my own efforts with the bees, our prairies and cropped fields, and about the dairies and the larger farming industry. Margaret Mead would have taken notice.

In Iowa, surrounded by farms and struggle and life and death, rather than crowds of distracting noisy people and their overwhelming busyness, I was finally able to get to work organizing my writing and explore the file cabinet of my life experiences. My rural setting unpacked me from the insulation that built up in my urban life and freed me to acknowledge and accept that I am indeed part of the natural world.

My time in the Midwest led to my recently published book. I became less averse to grief and death and was able to write about my experience closing the estates of four beloved family members. My book, *Ghost or Guardian, A Guidebook for the Pre-Dead, Do these things before you die so your heirs won't hate you later*, is a practical and humorous guide to leaving a legacy as a guardian of your family rather than a haunting ghost. It is about more than documents and clutter, but also family dynamics and practical issues that can be difficult, confusing, and even tortuous for those you leave behind. You may think your people know where everything is they will need to tidy up your mortal farewell, but will they remember? Will they disagree? Can you help them or do you intend to deliberately torture them? I wrote the book going through difficult times and tossed it in the file cabinet where it stayed until this season of my life, which is retirement from my agricultural work and corporate tasks to a move closer to family and a new opportunity to chart my own course.

I am an author now. I always wanted to do this creative work, and I am figuring it out and doing it with newfound resources and support from others with experience. I value and nurture my new network of support because I am aware of my persistent insecurities and aware of tools I need to sharpen. The role of storytelling in our modern world continues to evolve in form and importance but the past will always have power to inform the future and without telling our stories we devalue our very existence.

I was stunned at the reaction I received at an initial reading of the introduction to my book. My writing struck a chord with complete strangers. I offer something to others from my experiences that may bring them help, joy, relief, or guidance. Our valued shared experience is vital for a better future for all of us. If we don't value our legacy and our footsteps wash away without trace in the sand, were we ever here? Have we left any foundation for future generations to build upon?

I worked with a colleague in the dairy industry from China who spoke about his need to rush to succeed since his government mandated that he had to retire by age fifty to make room for the younger generation. Unimaginable for a person like me on a winding road to fulfillment. Artificially imposed time constraints by ourselves or others undermine our ability to find our way and reach imagined destinations. Every author in this book has taken a journey that did not involve time lost, but time well spent gaining experience and knowledge. We have reclaimed purpose with the time we invested in our own unique preparation for our new successes.

I am proud to be a member of a cadre of talented women who enthusiastically signed on to tell our stories of success, resilience, and powerful careers frequently working for organizations we did not control. What is different now for me and others is that we are grabbing the reins, making plans, succeeding or stumbling, but charting our own course to destinations that we choose. This course is not for everyone; but able, self-directed, and motivated people of any gender or generation can take charge of their lives and we aim to encourage with our examples.

What and when is retirement today for people who are healthy, active, used to being productive members of society and who have skills and experience that are valuable? After a certain age we need not be stuck idling as we wait to be plowed under. Health, energy, resources and enthusiasm are the drivers of what happens next after a layoff, downsizing or retirement; but we need not be irrelevant if we don't want to be.

Today I am as happy and productive as I have ever been professionally and personally. Working on my laptop, developing my marketing strategy, rummaging in my file cabinet for my next project, and developing new relationships in support of this activity is the game I have chosen, and I am still in the game and moving forward.

We are contributing. We all offer something of value in our fields of endeavor. The game would be diminished without us. Come join us. We need you too. Let's play.

INTRODUCTION TO
JENNIFER PETERS

Jen is an accomplished Life Sciences marketing strategist and brand leader. Over the course of her career, she has held positions in marketing, new product development and has been a team leader supporting over 25 product launches. Jen's work ethic and drive to help others in need started at a young age as the youngest in a family that struggled with mental health issues. Her admiration for her father, a WWII veteran who started his own business, motivated her to start her own successful strategic and creative consultancy serving private equity funded specialty pharmaceutical start-ups. She has built an incredible network that she leverages to help others. Over the last 15 years Jen has focused her career on oncology and rare disease. Her calming voice and self-deprecating personality has helped her become an accomplished moderator and interviewer of patients and caregivers. She resides in Chicago with her husband and beloved yellow lab Oliver. She is most proud of her grown daughter who shares her love of animals and helping people.

Find Your Me-Suite

Bam! Splat! Plink!

The recording of my three-year-old self reveals a lot of about me.

"No," I declare! "I will do it myself!"

You can hear my mom rustling with the recorder and sighing; then the recording stops.

I was born to excel and be independent. A midwestern girl raised by parents who survived the Great Depression. My father, Lloyd, returned from WWII without saying a word about what he experienced. He put his training and hands to good use and opened a tool-and-die business. My mother, Maybelle, and her twin sister, Marilyn and their family lived a mile away. Like most twins they had a special connection yet a deeply competitive one.

Marilyn went to college, but Maybelle didn't. Marilyn was an office manager, had three children, and her husband was a senior executive at a large moving company. Maybelle was a frustrated stay-at-home mom who promptly set the table at 6:00 pm even though dad never came home until after 7:30 pm.

Growing up I was acutely aware that my mother wanted the life and career that her twin sister had. Marilyn's kids went to college and launched high profile careers in publishing and TV. My brother and sister never went to college, and their adolescent and young adult years were fraught with challenges and social embarrassments. Then there was me the baby.

I was a surprise second-lifer baby as my mother often told her friends. Maybelle told everyone I was the result of a delicious home cooked French meal featuring French onion soup, coq au vin and chocolate mousse.

The pictures and old videos tell the story of how much I was loved. Everyone clambered to hold me and smile at the camera. I was a delight, and all the relatives fawned over me. Tommy my brother was fifteen years older and my sister Sue was ten years older than me. At a young age I picked up on my mother's deep sense of disappointment about our family compared to other families. This yearning for what others had was imprinted onto me at an early age.

Tommy was, well, different, and Sue was Daddy's little girl. She had no motivation or a compass. My mother was an unhappy person and resented my father for his commitment to his business. Because of this I strived hard to make her and other people happy. I adored my parents and I was focused on making them proud. I did this by excelling at everything and anything I attempted.

My drive to be perfect came from several places. First, I respected my hard-working, entrepreneurial father. Second, my mother who inspired my love of reading, photography and discovery expressed everyday her disappointment for not having pursued a higher education and a career like her sister. There is a third reason, a much darker one, influenced by the pervasive mental health issues of my older siblings and of course the stigma associated with mental illness.

Tommy's schizophrenia symptoms started the year he turned eighteen. The stress and havoc that comes with this horrible disease is unmatched. Maybelle couldn't live with the neighbors watching when the police showed up on our doorstep. To hide ourselves and our troubles away we moved to a rural town when I was five. The move increased my father's commute which made him even later for dinner.

Tommy was in and out of hospitals. Late night phone calls and threats of suicide dominated my parent's lives. Dad was always bailing him out in some way. One day he was confronted by an angry landlord because my brother had set a fire in his apartment. Sue got pregnant in high school to a hippy anti-war protester who used a swath of the American flag to patch a hole in the seat of his jeans. This guy was my dad's nightmare embodied.

As the baby, I carried the weight of the family dysfunction, and I felt the burden of being my parents' last hope for a normal and successful child. I had to fix everything and do something—anything—to make my parents proud and happy.

My straight A's were paired with lettering in four sports. I did the household chores and heavy yard work to spare my aging parents. I was terrified that my parents would die before I grew up. This fear of losing my parents early fueled my desire to work hard and earn money. I worked as a photographer and had a byline for the sports section of our local paper. And I was going to college to pursue a photojournalism degree.

Choosing the right college was not easy because I was shy. Today, friends and colleagues find this hard to believe, but I was. I applied to Michigan, Michigan State, Ferris State, and two smaller private colleges Albion and Alma. The bigger schools frightened me, so I was about to commit to Alma College when Aunt Marilyn begged me to check out her alma mater Indiana University in Bloomington, Indiana. I applied out of a sense of obligation but the idea of being so far away from my family was almost a non-starter. That fateful trip to IU was the first of many situations and opportunities that I fell into that launched my pursuit of a path of acceptance.

Being terribly homesick my freshman year, I threw myself into my studies and kept to myself. I was friends with several young women in the dorm and when they decided to join sororities in their sophomore year, I wasn't sure what to do because I didn't even know anything about the Greek system let alone understand the concepts of rush and pledging.

And even though I was shy, that desire to be accepted and pursue what my peers were chasing kicked in. I wanted to be accepted and follow the path that others were on. This is the first time I started chasing other people's dreams, and it was the first of many.

Like my girlfriends I did sorority rush week. I went through rush and decided to "suicide" the Theta house, meaning I went all in instead of having other sorority picks, because it was where my close girlfriends were pledging. I was warned it was rare to get in as a non-legacy, but my desire to be accepted was a big driving force. No surprise: I didn't get in the Theta house and I was devastated.

Later in my sophomore year I discovered women like me in the Gamma Phi sorority. Despite the heartbreak of being rejected by the Thetas, the most prestigious sorority known for studious young women from pedigreed families, pledging Gamma Phi was where I was meant to be because you could be different and accepted. You didn't have to fit the same mold. Some of my most treasured life-long girlfriends are Gamma Phis. There are about a dozen of us who vacation together, host euchre weekends in our respective cities, attend our children's weddings and play golf together.

While at IU I wanted to work because it I wanted to be independent, and I felt guilty that my parents were funding my out-of-state tuition. I worked in the kitchen in the dorm and was the campus Greek party photographer. I also worked for the college paper and yearbook.

Ring. Ring.

The phone on the wall wailed into my sorority room.

With a huff I unfolded myself from the bed and answered.

"Hello?"

"Hey Jen," it was mom. Her voice was shaky, and I knew something was wrong.

"What is it?" I nearly shouted. "Is dad okay?"

They found suspicious cells in my father's bladder, but the doctors said it was under control with monitoring and routine procedures to keep the cells at bay. My fierce loyalty and adoration for my father influenced another important decision and that was to also minor in business. Although, I didn't have any desire to live in Detroit and run a tool and die business. It was part of his legacy; so out of sense of obligation and loyalty I was determined to carry on the family name and the business he built, if needed.

Even though I thought marriage and children were not in my future, I met my future husband the beginning of my senior year. Although we really didn't have much in common other than a love of sports, we both wanted to pursue our careers and not have children. Dad had cancer and needed surgery, but he delayed surgery because he wanted to walk me down the aisle. I returned from my honeymoon and sat in a hospital waiting room for hours hoping the surgery would eradicate the offending disease. The surgery was unsuccessful, and my father refused radiation and chemotherapy.

My hero was gone in six months.

My dad's passing fueled my desire for career success because I knew he was watching from above. In his final days he sold the business and left everything to my mom. I wasn't called on to run his business. Even though sorority life brought me out of my introverted shell, I was still shy, however I joined the ranks of many of my classmates and headed to big dreams in Chicago.

My pulse raced and my nerves tingled when I walked down Michigan Avenue; the energy was new and exciting. I pursued opportunities at the acclaimed Chicago Tribune, the rival newspaper the Chicago Sun Times. I was a stringer, an unpaid intern, photographer for both papers. My husband was an unpaid videographer. One of us had to make money so I snatched up the first available job which was a traveling baby photographer.

Every Monday I picked up my equipment, film and assignment. My territory was Northern Illinois, all of Wisconsin, and parts of Iowa and Indiana. I photographed babies and children at the local Kmart from 8:00 AM to 8:00 PM. The hours were long, and the lines were too, especially in preparation for the holidays. After one long day of bending down to get newborns to smile, I thought to myself *I didn't go to college to do this line of work* so I quit and looked for another job more aligned with my college training. However, now I can make any baby or young child smile!

Next, I thought I hit the jackpot when I landed a photography position at a prestigious studio Stuart Rodgers that catered to the rich, famous and even infamous families of the North Shore and Chicago. It was here that I realized that although I had a good eye and timing my technical skills were not strong enough to make a solid living in photography. My customer relationship and new business selling skills revealed themselves and I was off to the races.

I enjoyed interacting with people and I found pleasure in seeing the joyful response to a loved one's captured photo. Finding new customers and growing the business energized me. I found myself on the outside looking into the lives of wealthy people and this drove me to want more. I chased my customers dreams of wealth and found my own financial success when I fell into an opportunity that catapulted me into the pharmaceutical industry. It is a profession that I have been honored to be a part of for the majority my career.

The Abbott Pharmaceutical division was like a start-up, small and entrepreneurial, a culture made for me. It is where I cut my teeth and learned marketing and where I met some amazing women who are still dear friends. We were all young starting our professional lives and personally looking at the future that included marriage and children. I supported multiple brands working in the in-house marketing communications department. I admired the product managers and wanted to be like them. When I got my chance to work in new product planning, I threw myself into the role and worked ridiculous hours because I wanted to achieve what my peers were achieving as I chased their dreams.

I had always thought I would build a successful career and forgo having children even though I preferred the company of children over adults sometimes. My husband also declared he never wanted children for other reasons. We were having fun being a dual-income-no-kids couple, and my career was taking off, when during a routine gynecological exam, doctors discovered some dysplastic cells; and for the next five years I had laser surgeries to remove the cells to prevent cancer.

At the same time my mother was diagnosed with Alzheimer's, and I had to make the painful decision to put her in a nursing home. Shortly thereafter while riding the train into the city I thought I'll probably outlive my husband and wondered who will take care of me when I get old. Nostalgia also washed over me, and I thought of my father, and I wondered who would pass on the family name. Perhaps the proverbial biological clock was also ticking as I was turning thirty that year but whatever it was, I decided that I *did* want children.

A few months later, on a ski trip with friends, while we were on a chair lift, my husband declared to me that he too would like to have a least one child. A few months later I was pregnant! Our daughter Hayley has been the greatest gift and the greatest sense of accomplishment for me over anything I've achieved in my career. Like many of my girlfriends I was about to face the challenge of balancing a career and being a mother.

I never felt on par with my peers, I wanted to be like my successful girlfriends both professionally and personally. From the outside looking in it looked like they had perfect careers, marriages, and children. My ever-present sense of never feeling like I measured up only intensified when my husband left me without warning when our daughter was two years old. I was a single mom juggling a busy career and the daily appointments with occupational and speech therapists to address my daughter's special needs.

Like I did with earlier setbacks I leaned in and worked harder. In hindsight I'm not sure this was the right strategy, but it was the only one I knew. Unfortunately, during this time, my desire to achieve the life my peers and friends had intensified. I often felt like I was circling outside of their orbit and chasing someone else's dreams. Fortunately, fate was about to prevail and change my life in more ways than one.

My time at Abbott was fulfilling until it wasn't. The culture and leadership changes and my pending divorce motivated me to take a leap of faith and join another start-up venture. A medical advertising agency, GSW in Columbus Ohio, aggressively pursued me, which is always a nice feeling; and I wanted a change of scenery and an opportunity to help build something.

I was employee number sixty-five and the only female vice president on the executive leadership team. Hayley, my daughter, was six when we moved to Ohio. Our dog Alf and a gerbil Billy joined the adventure to a new city. I threw myself into work. I rose in the ranks and became the first female Executive Vice President responsible for tremendous growth year over year.

We built a thriving agency and after nine years the company was sold and the benefits of working for a privately held organization evaporated as did my motivations. My time in Columbus was fulfilling: I made incredible friends and I met my new partner Phil, and was embraced by his extended family. I wanted to get back to Chicago and Phil was happy to venture outside of Columbus after he graduated from The Ohio University with a PhD in semi-conductor physics. In 2008 during the housing market crash we packed up our things with two dogs now and moved into a rental in Glenview, Illinois so my daughter could finish high school in a school that could support her special needs.

From one of the bedrooms in our rental I started my own strategic creative agency. Self-funding a start-up company in 2008, during the housing crash, being burdened by credit card debt, was not great timing. I knew my father would have been disappointed that I got into credit card debt, but I know he would have overlooked this misstep because he would have been so proud to see me follow in his entrepreneurial footsteps. This challenge turned into an opportunity to tighten my belt. I set a goal to be debt-free in two years and I did. Living debt free is hugely rewarding and freeing.

When I reached out to potential clients, many were past Abbott colleagues who were now C-suite leaders of start-up private equity-funded specialty pharmaceutical companies. I was humbled by the advice I received when I would ask Should I do this? Can I do this? and one executive said of course you should: you have built a strong brand, you are great at what you do, and people know you would drive through walls for them which is my people pleasing hallmark.

He was right, my brand has always been about working hard and smart on behalf of my clients. I also have a passion for helping clients find a uniquely differentiated position and never waiver which is why I named my company Brandzone with the playful tagline Find It, Keep It inspired by the children's rhyme *finders, keepers, losers, weepers*.

As I built my business, I discovered the importance of networking. I have become known as a great connector both in business and in my personal life connecting women with other women professionally and personally. Over the course of sixteen years, I was finally on my own path, and not chasing someone else's dreams.

I worked hard to build a successful business, logging long hours, and sacrificing personal home life, regretfully not always being there for Hayley. Thankfully she has forgiven me. Like my father, I provided not only for my family, but I provided work for many talented freelance project managers, designers, writers, editors, web designers, programmers, photographers, and videographers.

Starting my own company took guts and a fearless approach to finding clients and building these relationships into recurring organic assignments and growth. Finally, I was doing what I was destined to do, and on my terms, no one else's. It took decades, but I focused on what made me happy and leveraged my special powers. I don't regret any of the stops and pivots along my odyssey. My life and career choices and experiences span thirty-plus years and continue.

And I am not done yet. I recently decided to seek out one more fulfilling opportunity by going back to my roots and pursuing a marketing role at a biotech company focused on rare diseases, which has been my passion for the last fifteen years. I found my way to the Me-Suite and for me it's more rewarding than the C-Suite.

As I reflect on my life's journey thus far, I know I always tried my best, helped others along the way and found my tribe. I do wish I had not been so hard on myself and taken on too many of my family's burdens, but then again it made me what I am and shaped my career choices, which for the most part have been good ones.

My greatest accomplishment has been my daughter Hayley; and when she reads this, I hope she will understand me a little bit better and will be proud of me as much as I am proud of her, because she is the most beautiful and kind person I know. I've also been blessed with finding my soul mate, Phil, albeit later in life.

Phil is also my best friend and has supported every one of my decisions and tells me almost every day how proud he is of me and how amazed he is by my accomplishments. Oh, and I would be remiss if I didn't acknowledge my closest girlfriends, you know who you are.

You have brought so much joy to my life. As women,

girlfriends are so important especially the older we get. Cultivate women friendships both personally and professionally. We must do better to help each other achieve our career and personal goals. Don't be competitive with other women; be inspiring and supportive. Don't accept mediocrity, but don't step on a woman to achieve your goal: there are enough men who do that. Help other women find their path without tamping down their spirit. Not everyone is destined for the C Suite.

I know now that I spent too much time measuring myself by my career achievements not by life achievements. I spent too much time chasing other people's dreams. Be careful to not seek validation only from your career goals and accomplishments. Seek a life-work balance and find the joy in spending time with friends and family. Time is fleeting and you can't ask for a do-over.

I write my anthology chapter at a point of fulfillment and satisfaction because I no longer compare my accomplishments, my failures or my family to others. I wish I never did, but again I try not to dwell on what could have been, or what I should have done, or regret anything. No matter your age or where you are in your career—please be kind to yourself, take calculated risks and don't regret decisions that may lead you down an unexpected road. Your path will most likely not be linear but curvy, and you may accumulate some blemishes along the way and that's ok.

Embrace the blemishes and count on the silver linings that will always be there when you are dealt an unexpected blow. Be yourself, be authentic, and be kind to others along the way because the power of community is a life force.

Like in golf when you create a divot, just replace it. Follow your own path not the path that others may be on or that are deemed the status quo. Challenges are the building blocks to the foundation of your beautiful house. Find happiness in the curves, embrace the hand you are dealt, and help others along the way.

Find your Me-Suite.

INTRODUCTION TO
WENDI O. BROWN

Wendi O. Brown is a retired U.S. Army Lieutenant Colonel with over two decades of distinguished and decorated service, including combat deployments, post-9/11 assignments at the Pentagon, and strategic planning roles supporting U.S. Africa Command, U.S. European Command, and NATO operations. She played a vital role in advancing joint readiness and cyber-integrated planning through contributions to initiatives like Combined Joint All-Domain Command and Control (CJADC2) and NATO's premier communications interoperability exercise, Steadfast Cobalt. A summa cum laude graduate, she holds two Master of Science degrees in Cybersecurity, including a specialization in Cyber Intelligence, from programs recognized by the National Security Agency and the Department of Homeland Security. Today, she continues to serve national security as a Department of Defense contractor at U.S. Cyber Command, bringing expertise in cyber operations, strategic logistics, and high-stakes crisis response.

Beyond her government service, Wendi is the founder of iSupportYou, LLC, a strategic advisory firm dedicated to helping visionary leaders execute with precision in high-pressure domains. More about her work can be found at www.isupportyoullc.com.

Profit Powerhouse

YOU ARE THE PROFIT POWERHOUSE: SEASONED LEADERS FROM THE BATTLEFIELD DRIVE COMPETITIVE EDGE AND PROFITS

"You are a lamb in a lion's world," my senior office, a U.S. colonel stated.

At first, I was shocked and didn't know how to process that information. This conversation happened early in my military career, and he went onto share important information that shaped how I approached my work. He warned that unless I learned to handle intense pressure and assert my strength, the very system I served would break me. That conversation awakened something deep within me. From that point, I focused on not only molding my career but my identity. I learned to move with intention, to lead with conviction, and to carry a quiet power that needed no permission. What could have crushed me became the very ground I rose from.

That inner shift laid the foundation for every bold decision I made from that point forward.

WHY TRUST WENDI: THE GROUND I ROSE FROM

My Formula for Career and Self-Success

After completing a prestigious veteran internship at Goldman Sachs, I set my sights on a military assignment in Germany. As an Army Reservist, I understood how competitive military orders to Europe were. I applied with strategic intent, and I was selected.

What began as a one-year deployment became an eight-year tour, serving at both U.S. European Command and U.S. Africa Command. Each year, I had to requalify and prove my value. I never left that to chance. I developed a strategy to remain indispensable.

To stay ahead of evolving mission demands, I pursued advanced education in an emerging industry. First, I earned a Master of Science in Cybersecurity from the University of Maryland Global Campus, graduating summa cum laude. Then I advanced even further, earning a second Master of Science in Cybersecurity with a specialization in Cyber Intelligence from the Utica University, graduating summa cum laude. Utica University's Master in Science in Cybersecurity is formally recognized by the National Security Agency (NSA) and Department of Homeland Security as a National Center of Academic Excellence in Cyber Defense (CAE-CD).

This was not just about credentials. It was a deliberate investment and a strategic alignment of my military service with emerging cyber warfare capabilities. It secured my operational role year after year and positioned me to lead at the intersection of global defense and cyber intelligence.

During my military assignments in Europe, I intentionally sought out high-level engagements to deepen my strategic alignment not only with the United States, but with NATO member nations. I understood that influence in modern warfare required more than technical skill. It demanded multinational collaboration, operational awareness, and trust across allied forces.

For several consecutive years, I was invited to participate in premier NATO engagements, including the NATO Maritime Interdiction Operational Training Center (NMIOTC) Annual Security Conference, the NMIOTC Annual Cybersecurity Conference, and the NATO Center of Excellence for Integrated Air and Missile Defense (IAMD) Conference. These recurring invitations reflected a growing trust in my ability to bridge cyber strategy with coalition operations across international defense networks.

With decades of service at the highest levels of the U.S. military, I executed high-impact strategies across joint military commands and advised on decisions with global consequences. I delivered measurable impact at the Pentagon, U.S. European Command, U.S. Africa Command, and in combat with U.S. Forces Afghanistan and NATO's International Security Assistance Force (ISAF). In recognition of my mission-critical results and distinguished achievements, I have received some of the highest military honors, including the Bronze Star Medal, two Defense Meritorious

Service Medals, Non-Article 5 NATO Medal, Global War on Terrorism Expeditionary Medal, NATO ISAF Medal (International Security Assistance Force) and several others.

My responsibilities routinely provided strategy development, risk management, and crisis management, to execute national and international critical missions for U.S. interests throughout Europe, Middle East, and Africa.

YOUR LEGACY IS YOUR LEVERAGE. USE IT.

In today's competitive and disruptive business environment, traditional risk management and consulting recommendations do not suffice. Confidence without experience is a liability that can quickly erode profit margins. This is why C-suite executives and business leaders cannot rely on spirited youthful energy that is untested theories or unproven strategies. What they need are strategic foresight that others cannot see and then proven precise execution based on the strategic foresight – hallmarks of leaders who have navigated uncertainty and emerged stronger on the other side. And where can these qualities be found? In professionals over the age of fifty!

Unfortunately, seasoned professionals, especially over the age fifty, are often seen as obsolete, outdated, and old – better known as dinosaurs. They are underestimated in today's fast-paced, youth-centric corporate culture. However, the secret weapon to a *covert competitive edge* is to hire relevant professionals over this milestone age because they are not liabilities, they are the ultimate assets.

Like seasoned military commanders, they bring a wealth of experience, discipline, and operational mastery to the table. They possess the unique ability to turn chaos into clarity and uncertainty into unstoppable growth. You don't need a military background to understand the battlefield of business, you need the skills, wisdom, and right approach that comes from decades of experience.

KEY DIFFERENTIATORS

In every high-stakes operation, whether on the battlefield or in the boardroom, the most seasoned leaders are the ones called to lead. When chaos erupts, when markets shift, and when companies face complex challenges, organizations don't turn to the inexperienced, they turn to those who have weathered storms before. They've seen the patterns, navigated the pitfalls, and emerged stronger each time. They are the ones who recognize the patterns beneath the chaos, and who know instinctively which levers to pull when everything is on the line.

Despite this truth, many fifty-plus professionals find themselves systematically overlooked, undervalued, or prematurely pushed toward retirement paths. They encounter subtle and not-so-subtle biases and preferences in hiring processes.

That's not just wrong. It's dangerous thinking that threatens organizational resilience and sustainable profitability.

Today's business environment doesn't need more noise; it needs navigators with calibrated compasses. Organizations don't need trend-chasers perpetually distracted by the next shiny innovation; they need trusted decision-makers. And most critically, they don't need inexperience disguised as innovation; they need expertise that cuts through complexity and deliver consistent results.

The ability to anticipate challenges and see around corners? That comes with experience—the kind earned through navigating multiple market corrections and industry disruptions.

The confidence to lead with authority? That's the result of decades in the trenches, making high-consequence decisions and living with their outcomes.

The skill to transform risks into rewards? That's the strategic advantage that only comes from having weathered perfect storms and emerged stronger.

Consider how a seasoned professional over fifty whether from a military background, corporate leadership, or entrepreneurial ventures embodies these qualities. After decades in complex, high-profile, high-pressure environments, they bring unparalleled leadership clarity and organizational resilience. Their grasp of risk assessment, crisis response protocols, and team cohesion strategies have been refined through thousands of real-world applications. This level of critical judgment younger professionals simply cannot match, regardless of their technical proficiency or academic credentials.

Here's why businesses should actively seek professionals with this level of experience.

Key Differentiation #1:
Leadership & Decision-Making an Edge to Leverage

Effective Leadership and Decision-Making are about making the *right decisions at the right time using the right people and right resources (systems, processes, and technology)*. In the corporate world, this methodical approach is invaluable.

Character Traits to Effective Leadership and Decision-Making: (use landmine language)

- **Corporate Chief Strategist:** Design strategies to execute business strategic initiatives
- **Corporate Landmine Detector:** Identifies potential risks and pitfalls.
- **Corporate Landmine Diffuser:** Crafts methods to eliminate dangers.
- **Corporate Landmine Mitigator:** Execute contingency plans

Comparison: The Younger Professional's
Passion vs. The Veteran's Precision

While younger professionals often demonstrate admirable energy, their decision-making can be underdeveloped and driven more by a desire to establish professional credibility or achieve immediate visibility than by sound strategic considerations. This tendency toward action over reflection can lead to well-intentioned but costly miscalculations when complex variables aren't fully considered.

In contrast, a seasoned professional who has led organizations through multiple tough situations has a healthy skepticism toward quick fixes and universal solutions. Their focus gravitates naturally toward comprehensive analysis, risk considerations, and long-term consequences precisely the qualities essential when navigating high-stakes business environments where the margin for error grows increasingly thin. Their decision-making incorporates not just data analytics but the contextual wisdom to interpret those analytics.

Key Differentiation #2: Strategic Vision, Risk Management and Navigating Uncertainty

What distinguishes seasoned professionals from their younger counterparts is their developed capacity to anticipate potential system failures before warning indicators appear in dashboards or reports. A leader with extensive military experience can analyze situations with exceptional depth, seeing beyond surface metrics to understanding underlying dynamics.

Comparison: Instinct vs Insight
While younger professionals may demonstrate impressive data literacy and analytical capabilities, they frequently lack contextual knowledge. Their risk assessments, while technically sound, often fail to account for human factors, geopolitical considerations, and historical parallels that aren't captured in datasets.

However, a seasoned executive or military leader has witnessed and experienced multiple cycles of disruption and possesses the ability to identify emerging threats. Their risk assessment incorporates both quantitative models and qualitative judgment enabling them to act proactively rather than merely responding to established trends. This ability represents an invaluable organizational capability that can preserve capital during downturns and position companies advantageously during recovery phases.

Businesses that fail to prioritize experienced leadership will always struggle to anticipate what's next

Key differentiation #3:
Crisis Management, Adaptability,
Remaining Steady Under Pressure

When crises strike whether competitive, regulatory, or macroeconomic organizational response quality correlates directly with leadership experience. Having faced genuinely consequential scenarios throughout their careers', seasoned professionals have developed psychological resilience and decisional clarity under extreme pressure. This emotional equilibrium enables them to navigate organizations through turbulence with measured confidence rather than reactive panic.

Seasoned professionals have the ability to:

- Maintain **mental clarity** under extreme pressure.
- Execute **rapid problem-solving** without panic.

- Turn **crises into opportunities** by making calculated moves.

This level of resilience is critical in today's volatile business environment. Organizations need leaders who don't just survive under pressure but thrive in it.

Comparison: The Inexperienced vs The Battle-Tested
Smart younger leaders may project confidence in theoretical crisis scenarios, but without direct experience managing genuine threats, many struggle when confronted with the psychological weight of significant decisions affecting thousands of lives. In contrast, the battle-tested executive has developed emotional mechanisms specifically calibrated for high-stakes scenarios. They've established personal protocols for maintaining strategic thinking when others become tactically reactive. This capacity for clear-headed analysis represents perhaps the most valuable yet least quantifiable asset a leader can bring to an organization.

**Key Differentiation #4:
Emotional Intelligence,
Conflict Resolution and Diplomacy**

The emotional intelligence of seasoned professionals represents another differentiating advantage, developed through decades of managing diverse personalities, navigating complex organizational politics, and resolving deeply entrenched conflicts. A military leader brings diplomatic skills, contextual sensitivity, and proven capabilities essential for building coalition support and maintaining organizational cohesion. Battle-tested professionals excel in:

- **Conflict resolution:** Defusing tensions before they escalate. Creating a work environment of solidarity and cohesion.
- **Diplomacy:** Navigating complex relationships with tact and authority. Having the ability to influence outcomes.
- **Team leadership:** Building trust, morale, and respect among diverse teams. Pushing employees passed their comfort zones.

Comparison: Reactive Tension vs. Diplomatic Adaptability
While having impressive technical capabilities and fresh viewpoints, many younger professionals react spontaneously in emotionally charged situations often reacting to workplace tensions with either avoidance behaviors or confrontational approaches. Their communication styles, while direct, may lack the situational adaptability required to navigate sensitive stakeholder relationships or multi-cultural business environments.

By contract, experienced executives and military leaders have developed finely calibrated emotional sensors that detect subtle shifts in organizational mood, identify potential alliance structures, and recognize unspoken concerns beneath surface discussions. They understand when to apply pressure versus when to release tension, and how to create psychological safety during turbulent times, skills that prove invaluable when leading diverse teams through uncertainty or managing complex external partner relationships.

STRATEGIC PLAYBOOK FOR BATTLE TESTED LEADERS

Section 1: Strategy Developer: The Skills That Make You Irreplaceable

- **Command-Level Thinking:** The most valuable executives demonstrate an ability to rapidly make complex decisions systematically and with clarity. This command-level thinking separates mere managers from true organizational leaders, as it enables decisive action in situations where perfect information remains unavailable and time pressures demand immediate responses.

- **Situational Awareness:** Beyond individual decision quality, seasoned professionals demonstrate exceptional situational awareness, the ability to detect meaningful trends within market environments that indicate emerging opportunities or threats. This capacity for early pattern recognition comes from experience in understanding the subtle indicators that precede major shifts.

- **Crisis-Tested Leadership:** The ability to remain steady when others panic. In times of crisis, the most experienced leaders are the ones who can keep their cool. They've been through tough situations before and know how to navigate them with poise and precision. The calm confidence such leaders project creates cascade effects throughout organizations, enabling teams to maintain discipline when competitors become reactive or paralyzed by uncertainty.

Section 2: The Myth of the Expiration Date: Why Your Prime is Now

- **Dismantle Limiting Frameworks That Undermine ROI:** There is a prominent misconception that the value of seasoned professionals significantly lessens after a certain age. In other words, they represent a strategic liability for organizations operating in complex markets.

  Forward-thinking organizations have recognized this reality and have reevaluated their talent frameworks to prioritize judgment quality and proven adaptability over age. They understand that the most valuable organizational capability in volatile environments is strategic wisdom.

- **Top Value is Based on Executive Wisdom:** Executive wisdom, defined as the integration of analytical capacity, trend recognition, emotional intelligence, and ethical judgment, emerges as the critical differentiator. Leaders who have developed this wisdom through decades of practice bring irreplaceable capabilities to organizations navigating unprecedented opportunities.

- **Shape Industries and Boardrooms:** Far from representing sunset careers, many professionals in their fifth and sixth decades are driving organizational innovation and industry transformation. Their deep contextual knowledge combined with experience enables them to architect solutions across traditional boundaries and implement changes that would prove impossible for less established leaders.

Section 3: Conquer Your Career Evolution: Be the Ultimate Leadership Asset

- **Strategically Positioned for High-Impact Roles:** For experienced professionals seeking to maximize their market impact, strategic role selection proves essential. Board directorships represent perhaps the most direct application of executive wisdom in governance contexts. Executive advisory roles enable a similar impact through more flexible engagement models. Independent consulting practices provide another impactful channel for seasoned executives.

- **Master Executive Presence:** Stay visible, relevant, and in demand by demonstrating the strategic value that only comes with decades of experience. Battle-tested leaders don't chase trends; they evaluate them with precision while maintaining the fundamental leadership principles that drive sustainable results. Like seasoned military commanders, they know how to position themselves as the calm center in chaotic environments, showcasing their unique ability to see around corners and anticipate challenges before they emerge.

Section 4: AI Can't Replace Experience. It Needs It.

- **Experienced Professionals Transform Data Overload into Strategic Focus:** In a world overflowing with data and rapid shifts, it takes seasoned insight to identify what truly matters. Women who have spent decades leading through uncertainty know how to silence the noise and make clear, effective decisions. Their ability to cut through complexity and prioritize action is what turns chaos into measurable gains.

- **Battle-Tested Professionals Possess a Currency Machines Can't Create—Trust:** Revenue is not only earned through performance. It's sustained through relationships. Women over 50 often carry a depth of trust capital built through years of leadership, integrity, and consistent results. They are the ones who keep clients loyal, build cohesive teams, and stabilize organizations when disruption threatens to shake foundations.

- **Seasoned Professionals Anticipate What Others Don't See Coming:** Where others react, they anticipate. Years of leadership have sharpened their intuition, allowing them to identify early signals of change, avoid unseen pitfalls, and recognize new opportunities before the market catches on. This ability to stay steps ahead is not based on guesswork. It is the result of hard-earned wisdom that gives companies a powerful advantage.

While disruption grabs attention, it is seasoned clarity that drives financial results and transformative achievements. It is the ability to lead with precision, insight, and composure under pressure. Seasoned professionals bring a rare depth of judgment that cannot be rushed or replicated or threatened by AI. Their leadership is not based on theory. It is forged through decades of decision-making in high-stakes environments where outcomes mattered. They see what others miss, act before others react, and deliver results when others hesitate. For companies expecting sustainable growth, resilient teams, and bold transformation, experience is not just valuable. It is indispensable.

INTRODUCTION TO
NANCY HEDLUND

Nancy Hedlund is a senior global healthcare executive, advisor, and research scientist with over 30 years of experience at healthcare firms such as Astellas, Baxter, and Amerisource-Bergen. She holds a PhD in Public Health Sciences, focusing on Health Economics and Policy. In her consulting work, she merges scientific and policy expertise with strategic insight to foster innovation and enhance patient outcomes.

As Managing Director of MedNavigate, LLC, Nancy empowers biotech, medical device, diagnostics, and health IT companies to successfully launch new technologies and achieve market growth. She integrates research science, data analytics, clinical practice, and technology to identify opportunities for value demonstration and market differentiation. Since founding MedNavigate, she has effectively guided multiple organizations through funding rounds, FDA approvals, and product launches.

Nancy collaborates with life science companies to assess patient needs, evaluate provider delivery, and identify unmet market demands. She develops strategic evidence for pricing, health technology assessments, and reimbursement to enhance market access. Championing substance over style, Nancy's work exemplifies integrity, critical thinking, and a passion for patient impact through effective evidence strategies. She speaks at healthcare conferences, contributes to HEOR (health economics and outcomes research) journals, and mentors emerging professionals, focusing on patient-centered strategies and evidence-driven decision-making.

Nancy and her husband, Paul, are the parents of four grown children aged 25 to 32. She enjoys attending Pilates and yoga classes, gardening, and spending some time in the kitchen. Together, they live in Skokie, IL, and love taking day trips to downtown Chicago to experience everything the city has to offer.

The Final Pivot

Imprinted by Youthful Experiences Rural farm girl. Big family, second of six kids. Shy. Perfectionist. Limited economic means.

Money was always tight for my parents, in fact, tighter than I appreciated growing up. The table was always set with food, mostly from our own garden or produced locally. Out in the country, it was customary to purchase a quarter of a cow at a time from a local butcher to pack away in the deep freeze, so there was always meat and potatoes on the table but that was it, nothing fancy or extra.

The principles of responsibility and self-sufficiency were instilled at an early age. Watching younger siblings in the morning while our mom performed household chores, followed by free time in the afternoon. Helping with farm and garden tasks. I weeded rows and splashed white paint on the base of fruit tree saplings to reflect the sun and prevent uneven growth. We sewed and stuffed small satchels with human hair collected from the local barbershop to be attached to fruit tree saplings to deter deer from snacking on them. I produced enough of these satchels to purchase my high school class ring.

I was never an athlete, but I was crafty. I learned how to and liked to sew through a local 4-H program and competed my wares in the county fair. I fashioned doll clothes from store patterns and sold my output to my aunts for gifts for my younger cousins. I even hand-crafted the blazer I wore in my senior photo.

I turned sixteen in January of my sophomore year of high school and joined my sister waiting tables at a local restaurant. My family did not have the financial resources for travel on spring breaks, so I always picked up extra hours at the restaurant and treated myself to a shopping spree at the end of the week with my tips to update my wardrobe.

My eyes are set on college from a young age. I saw higher education as my ticket to a regular work schedule and the ability to take annual vacations. Initially, I thought I wanted to be a nurse, but a short stint through a nurse assistant training program changed my mind. I have always liked science and considered medical school, but I didn't have the resources or the encouragement of my family to pursue it. I also wasn't sure I wanted to be so hands-on with patients. Instead, I decided to pursue pharmacy and applied to the University of Michigan.

"Hello," the cheerful voice said. "I would like to speak to Nancy."

"This is she," I questioned.

"This is Janet from the University of Michigan," she continued. "We are happy to let you know that you are accepted into the PharmD program!"

I held my breath while my mind sped through the information.

"Wow! Thank you so much!"

I couldn't wait to tell my parents, my sister was on a full scholarship to Michigan State, now they would have another child in college! The celebration was short-lived, because a few weeks later, I received a letter informing me I would receive no financial aid. How might the school have the audacity to suggest my parents sell their farm to pay for my schooling.

Fortunately, my guidance counselor came through, and I landed at Ferris State with a scholarship and Pell Grant. Although disappointed, I was on my way. I was on the march to my B.S. in Pharmacy degree, following blindly in the footsteps of my uncle, who was a pharmacist. Overall, it was a good ride. I made some great friends in college and graduated at the top of my pharmacy school class.

EARLY CAREER

My first job out of college was as a hospital pharmacist at a large sprawling 1000 bed hospital in Detroit, Michigan. The hospital was much larger than the Grand Rapids hospitals where I completed my studies. The intravenous (IV) room was always bustling. This is where we prepared intravenous solutions for premature infants, chemotherapeutic regimens for cancer patients, and everything else in between. Running the night shift alone was terrifying.

During one of these early shifts, I received an order for an intraocular injection for a patient in the emergency department, which was new to me. The concentration on the order was specified in an unusual format, which meant I needed to figure out, in the middle of the night, how to convert from a mg/ml antibiotic starting concentration to the molar equivalent requested. The solution I was preparing would be injected right into someone's eye!

The more mature me now understands that there are several options I might have taken to receive support, including informing the medical resident that I am second-guessing myself on how to prepare the preparation he was requesting. Instead, I was flipping through reference texts to cross-check how to perform the calculation and prepare the solution as ordered, while everything else requiring my attention is falling behind. Lesson learned: ask for help.

I moved to Detroit, MI, following my graduation from Ferris State with a scholarship in hand to pursue a Pharm D. degree at Wayne State University, but my heart wasn't in it. After working side by side with the Pharm D's, going on clinical rounds with the doctors, and hanging out socially with recent Pharm D graduates employed at the same health system, I started questioning whether a clinical specialist career path was the right avenue for me. Although my school would be paid for, I needed money to pay rent. In addition, the used car I purchased while in high school was beyond repair. I needed to get a full-time job.

I dropped out of graduate school and returned to full-time employment. It was the first time I quit anything so significant, but I needed a break from constant studying and a paycheck to get back on my feet.

Back at the hospital, an inspirational supervisor with a MBA degree intrigued me. She approached challenges from a different perspective. A year later, I returned to my roots in Western Michigan, took a job at a local hospital, and started taking night classes via a satellite MBA program (virtual educational classes not yet a thing).

My best friend Carol from undergrad was into matchmaking and arranged for me to meet my now-husband of thirty-three years on a blind date.

"I have someone I think you should meet," Carol said with a sly grin.

"Who is he? How do you know him?"

"We went to grade school and high school together, and he just moved to Grand Rapids, himself," she paused to get my response. "He works in sales."

Knowing I was a bit shy and introverted, she offered to get a group together and go to a movie, then go for dinner and drinks afterward. I agreed and we hit it off.

Paul's grandfather owned an orchard, like my parents', which provided us common ground to discuss. Our romance was swift, and we married two years later. We both worked full-time while I continued taking evening classes, earning my MBA with distinction, five months before giving birth to our first child.

I never imagined how becoming a mother would transform me. I was career-oriented and pushed myself hard academically for a very long time. We didn't want our children in daycare full-time, so we agreed I'd hang on to my career by working part-time for a few years. Our perfect plan was to have two kids close together, and once they'd started pre-school, I'd hop back into full-time work and begin climbing the provincial career ladder.

The universe had other plans. Turns out my fertility wasn't a given. While Janessa came quickly, the second child, close in age to our first in my fictional life plan, was not in the cards. Paul and I endured multiple miscarriages, followed by a devastating stillbirth. I carried Morgan for thirty-seven weeks, learning her heart had stopped beating during a routine weekly OB appointment. My heart was racing. We were directed to the hospital for a complete ultrasound, although no one else seemed to be in a hurry. They already knew what the sonogram would confirm. Morgan was dead.

We were sent back home to gather our things and wait for a bed to open on the labor and delivery ward. I was induced, which turned out to be close to a 24-hour procedure. I delivered Morgan, vaginally, just like giving birth to any other child. Only she wasn't alive, she wasn't breathing, and quickly grew cold. Throughout the induction, I feared I would be scared to hold her. The opposite was true. They wrapped her in warm blankets, and I didn't want to let go. When they wheeled Morgan's little bassinet out of the room, it was the last time we saw her.

Instead of waking up in the middle of the night for feedings, we planned her funeral. However, there was no birth or death certificate. In the eyes of the law, Morgan wasn't a real person, as her heart ceased beating before, she could say hello to the outside world. That also meant her funeral expenses would come directly out of our pocket. Though we had a family life insurance policy, her life was not eligible.

The graveside service was beautiful. My sisters Cathy and Linda played the flute, and friends and family surrounded us. I no longer recall the name of the vocalist, but I remember her sweet voice entranced the small gathering. I sobbed the entire time. Sometimes quietly, sometimes with loud hiccups and snot, but I never stopped crying. My husband, Paul, was a little more stable. Neither of us had a clue as to what the grieving process had in store for us.

I share this very personal story with all of you, as I firmly believe our lives and careers are comprised of chapters. The loss of Morgan rattled me. It marked time. There was now a before and after Morgan. I wanted only a baby in my arms; nothing else mattered. My career was the last thing on my mind. Depression and fertility treatments became my reality. I was maniacally focused on having a baby. They shot me up with hormones, and everything we could get our hands on to try and make a baby.

Prior to Morgan's passing, I was employed by a regional

long-term pharmacy as a pharmacy consultant. This meant I routinely drove three hours away to perform chart reviews and medication audits at facilities within the territory I managed. Now I dreaded being that far away from our two-year-old daughter, Janessa. My husband also traveled hours from home for sales calls. We had backup plans in place should an emergency occur, but they were no longer good enough for me. *Another pivot.*

I landed a job as director of pharmacy services for a local lifecare retirement community. Our residents ranged from independent seniors to patients in skilled nursing facilities. We also supported homecare and hospice service lines. I started working five days a week, as it was just too painful to be at home. I knew my new gig didn't present a career ladder, although I was gaining valuable people management experience. I didn't care. I was thirty minutes from home, earning an income, and that is all that was important.

Two and a half years later, we were blessed with healthy twins. The pregnancy was rough, and I was required to take an early leave of absence, spending ten weeks confined to the couch to keep pre-term labor in check. I took an additional twelve weeks' leave to recover and get to know our new family. We located a fantastic daycare home, which enabled me to resume employment four days a week. I worked Monday and Tuesday, took Wednesdays off as a mom, and then went back on-site Thursday and Friday, with every third weekend call.

My newfound utopia lasted for a couple of years, prior

to the leadership of the organization deciding to close the pharmacy service line. New Medicare payment guidelines were enveloping long-term care, taking a hit on the profitability of our pharmacy. The retirement community decided to contract with an external service provider like the one I had previously worked with and discontinue their internal services, all while I was expecting our fourth child. Looking back now, young parenthood with four young kids, marked with periods of crushing grief, and muddled career changes, is an absolute blur. I have no idea how we survived it all.

With our new family officially complete, I joined the hospital sector for a second time, only this time on a part-time basis. With four kids seven and under, it's all that I can handle. The newly merged system director of pharmacy needed administrative support and was fond of my skills and work ethic from our prior time working together. I assumed the lead role for a grant-funded medication safety study and led the implementation of multiple pharmacy-related IT systems. I relished systems thinking along with the introduction of new innovative technologies. Though my role was half-time, I enjoyed the work I was doing.

Three years later, with our twins now attending school full-time, it was time for Paul and me to explore opportunities for me to jump back on the career ladder. The two most apparent paths for growth are taking on a hospital pharmacy department of my own or entering the external health tech industry. Either option meant leaving our home of thirteen years in Grand Rapids, Michigan. There was no related industry locally, and incumbent hospital leaders typically held on to their roles for twenty to thirty years, as there were few other opportunities for them in the local marketplace. *An exciting pivot.*

CHICAGO, HERE WE COME.

As the cards would have it, I accepted an offer with Amerisource-Bergen in 2004 for a product director role with their pharmacy automation division, ABTG, which included a relocation package to Chicago. Paul took a turn working part-time while returning to the classroom to earn a master's degree in education.

From ABTG, I migrated to Hospira, again allowing me to build a team. We worked with cutting-edge technology, enabling hospitals to upscale their medication infusion platforms and wirelessly pull data from hospital servers to understand safety performance. We preached safety and system value and helped our clients demonstrate ROI from their technology purchases.

CONSCIOUS RETOOLING

After five swift years at Hospira, the company entered a period of ongoing remediation on the product line my team was supporting, meaning all new product shipments to health systems are placed in indefinite hold. I witnessed a reduction in force across the device software development team the year prior, and rumors that the business line my team supported would be spun out are frequent. Conference and seminar budgets are non-existent, but tuition reimbursement was still intact.

I convinced my boss that taking a pharmacoeconomics course at a downtown university could help me retool the team. You see, our devices generated a substantial amount of data, and we wanted to demonstrate how using our technologies improved the performance of the hospital's staff and systems. Soon, a second and third class followed, the maximum allowed as a non-degree-seeking student. Meanwhile, remediation efforts stretch into a second year. Up to now, the company has not laid off anyone in my area of the company; however, I feared my position to be at risk. Another *pivot* was in order—was it crazy, returning to school full time in my mid-forties? I convinced myself there was no harm in applying to the university's PhD program. I got in!

With a tuition waiver and a teaching assistant (TA) contract in hand, I took a leave of absence from Hospira. The university graduate assistant wages are meager, and balancing a full-time class load with TA and family responsibilities turned out to be more burdensome than I expected. The support of my husband, who really stepped up on the home front, was critical in allowing me to pursue this new goal.

Despite the crazy hours, it was my sabbatical of sorts. I relished the invigorating conversations and the skills I was acquiring. I was counting on these new skills to guide me through the remainder of my employment career, and to one day provide me with the foundation to launch my own business.

LARGE PHARMA

While in grad school, I volunteered on a local nonprofit board, where a fellow board member was also a senior vice president of Human Resources at Baxter Healthcare Corporation. She respected my conduct during board meetings and introduced me to a hiring manager responsible for Baxter's health economics and market access functions. I interviewed and landed a job conducting real-world data studies and advising on strategy to support the corporation's hospital products division. Meanwhile, I began the grueling work of chipping away at dissertation research during evenings and weekends.

While at Baxter I worked on several exciting projects with amazingly talented people, honing my new portfolio of skills. My role allowed me to revisit topics from MBA school and marry them with health economics principles acquired during PhD studies. Albeit, three years in the company split in two, spinning off the biosciences division and restructuring the remaining core hospital products group. The cuts came suddenly. While my manager attempted to assure me that our group was safe, that was not the case. I plunged headfirst into dissertation work, determined to finish up with a small severance package to sustain us. I refused to let all those years of schoolwork and sacrifice be a waste. All but dissertation (ABD) was not an option for me.

With a clear runway in place for wrapping up my dissertation research, I took on consulting projects for supplemental income. It was rewarding to win contracts and cash checks for services rendered. At the same time, with my husband's meager teaching salary, two kids in college and a third about to get married, I went back inside when a full-time research director opportunity with a Japanese Pharmaceutical Company was offered to me.

I enjoyed my colleagues and learned significantly more about working with real-world data (RWD) – think claims data, electronic medical record data, lab data, etc. I even developed elementary programming skills in SQL. I worked on teams with some incredible people. However, the organization's hierarchical culture is challenging for me. As a pioneer and change agent at heart, I find the culture to be constricting.

The abrupt transition to working from home during the onset of the Covid-19 pandemic is challenging, particularly given the earlier reliance on face-to-face interaction. Communication is fractured, and despite my best efforts, I am falling behind. In addition, I am also being asked to take on additional tactical responsibilities and to rely on the members of the teams we are supporting to think strategically.

The pandemic allowed me to reassess what was important to me, particularly after all those years of grad school. When I returned to the classroom, I was motivated to equip myself with skills to market myself as a solopreneur. Though

I established an LLC several years earlier, my corporation had largely been a fallback for supplemental income. Was it time to fully launch my dream? What was holding me back? Was it time for another *pivot*?

LAUNCHING MEDNAVIGATE AS A FULL-TIME BUSINESS

Establishing a consulting business during a global pandemic presented a unique blend of opportunities and challenges. With working from home becoming the new norm, attracting business across a broader geography is now possible. On the flip side, the inability to network at trade shows has complicated the process of reconnecting with former contacts and establishing new relationships. People are active on LinkedIn but are also becoming fatigued with being online.

Determined to make it a go, I built a company website and reached out to everyone I knew online to announce my availability. The advantage of having previously worked for several companies with divested divisions is that I have former colleagues spread across various new companies. Contracting opportunities came along. Some I fulfilled on my own, and for others, I formed virtual teams. I made new friends and established working relationships with a network of complementary solopreneurs. In these early years of running my business, I thought less about what I wanted for my business and more about bringing in the next check.

I am now four years into running MedNavigate as a full-time business entity, with professional networks established across several mastermind groups, including HerCsuite®, ProNexus Advisory, and RxRoundtable. In addition, I am an active member of the International Society for Pharmacoeconomic Outcomes Research (ISPOR) and The Academy of Managed Care Pharmacy (AMCP) professional trade organizations. I've invested in traveling within the U.S. and internationally to attend industry conferences, participate in current events, and make new connections.

With a new executive branch of our government in place, the market is again reacting to several uncertainties. At the same time, periods of unrest could be paving the way for new opportunities. I recently delivered my tenth annual guest lectures to master's in biotechnology students at Northwestern University as a component of a regulatory sciences elective. This past week, I followed up with a coffee chat with a particular student who caught my attention.

"Thank you for making time to meet with me," Dhinal entreated. "I really enjoyed your lecture. I was impressed with how you presented with such confidence."

"Thank you! I am so happy you agreed to a coffee chat. Your questions entail more than five-minute response after class."

"Your background resonates with me," she continued. "I trained as a pharmacist in India before coming to the U.S. to pursue a Master's in Biotechnology Degree."

"I understand, I made many pivots in my career along the way," I smiled and shared. "Some made by choice and others imposed upon me."

Looking back, there is no way I could have predicted or even begun to recreate the series of steps across my career journey, multiple of which are lateral and involved learning a new industry. However, the learnings and experiences captured along the way have made me who I am today. The time spent working within hospitals and consulting to long-term care nursing facilities equips me with a strong appreciation of the responsibilities each clinical team member juggles during a shift. When counseling young people, I encourage them to find a role that interests them and learn as much as possible. Careers are full of *pivots.* There is no perfect way to get started.

In many ways, I feel like I am just beginning a journey toward what truly matters to me. For the longest time, I was either dealing with grief or playing it safe to support the financial needs of our family. With our four children now through college and with a mortgage recently paid, I have greater freedom to explore somewhat riskier endeavors. A challenge for me is to give myself this permission, to allow myself to take time to reinvent, without expending energy worrying about where the next project might come from. Only then will I truly understand what it might take to fully self-actualize.

REBRANDING- CARVING OUT MY NICHE

I started working with a marketing coach on refining my value proposition. I struggled for some time to articulate my company's purpose to people not entrenched in the field. If I can't explain it myself, how can I expect others to understand? It was time to focus my energies on what I do well, and to hire external talent to build my company's branding in a way that amplifies the experience and the power our virtual teams bring to the table.

A colleague and co-author, Laurie Wessels, has a saying `LOVE -LIKE-CAPABLE'. There are many things I am capable of that I don't necessarily enjoy doing. Rather, these types of projects are assignments that bring in a paycheck which is accompanied by mental exhaustion. I've come to realize that I earned the right to be selective in the types of assignments I accept.

I entered the life sciences industry later in my career, via a technical proficiency route. My age at entry compressed my runway time to climb the ladder. Add to that, all the reorganizations I navigated and the challenging nature of my career becomes obvious.

I understand that I do not need to let my past limit who I am today. My knowledge and professional experience make me a strategic asset, particularly to early and mid-stage companies that do not have a full roster of industry professionals on deck.

I started approaching my client conversations with this knowledge in mind. My conversations with colleague solopreneurs in my referral network come from that same place of strength and confidence. I recently helped a medical device company derive endpoints for inclusion in a clinical trial. These endpoints will establish data that equips the organization to communicate a compelling value story. Right now, I'm designing an economic model from the target customer viewpoint which will give investors a realistic basis for pricing decisions, an important component to upcoming fundraising efforts. Today I spent all day as an invited advisory board guest with a second medical device company, and enjoyed collaborating with fellow panelists, company board members and senior leadership as we evaluated commercialization strategy options. While the day was physically exhausting, I departed intellectually stimulated.

I am a valuable strategic asset with a unique set of expertise sought after in the pharmaceutical and med-tech industries.

VICTORY LAP

I was having breakfast with a well-established senior industry colleague. We were discussing options to advance our practice discipline. Midway in our conversation, my colleague stated: "Neither one of us is shy. It is easy for us to get out and talk to people."

I nearly fell off my chair, knowing the earlier career version of myself. You see, my colleague and I have known each other for less than a year, yet she sees and describes me as I carry myself today.

I am positioning myself as a health economics expert. A core service offering is to build out an economic justification for a viable price point for a technology in development. My differentiating factors are my professional experience base and the hand-curated virtual team of experts I bring to the table.

As a boutique consultancy, I offer flexibility which is hard to achieve in a larger firm. I ensure that each client is introduced to the experts they will be working with at the onset of each engagement.When we sign on, we onboard as virtual partners, committed to the success of the entire project or effort. Our vision is to be less of a vendor and more of an embedded collaborator.

Something new I am experimenting with is creating a low-cost market entry package to engage with early-stage companies that need strategic advice but are not yet ready to commit to a substantial investment in market access strategies and tactics.

While 2025 started out on the slow side, business has since picked up. I attribute this partially to the internal development work and partially to a new messaging approach. I'm not sure exactly how long I will continue to work, but I know I still have several good years ahead of me. I'm allowing myself to dream a little bigger and not let go. Today is about me and my dreams. It's about feeling fulfilled with purpose and impact while generating an income commensurate with my experience.

I've demonstrated resilience, overcome significant grief, and successfully balanced career and family responsibilities. I no longer need to walk the financial tightrope, nor fit into a narrow job description. With fewer external demands on my time, I focus my energy on doing things that truly fulfill me.

I am in the driver's seat, and I get to determine my future direction. I am not the same person I was at the various earlier stages of my life. I am wiser and more resilient, with experience across a multitude of industries to include health systems, health IT, medical device, pharma/biotech and diagnostics.

Some weeks I work a lot of hours, but it is my choice and on my terms. Running a consultancy along with serving as principal consultant is not simple or easy. Blending continuous business outreach with excellence of service delivery is challenging. The conscious retooling undertaken during my later forties is paying off, having equipped me with the knowledge and tools to launch and scale a business enterprise.

"What would you dream if you knew you couldn't fail?" Natalie Benamou, the coordinating author and sponsor of this book, asked.

I am still working on an answer to that question. I haven't allowed myself to think this way in the past, but maybe *now* is the time. It's not a question I need to answer overnight, but it is a question I owe myself the time to think about.

But for now, my team and I are going to continue to develop rigorous, evidence-driven strategies that empower our clients to secure investment, achieve regulatory approval, and sustain long-term success in the marketplace.

The final *pivot*: the future is mine to own, and I am embracing it.

INTRODUCTION TO
LIESL SCHMIDT

Liesl Schmidt is a financial executive, board leader, and transformation strategist with over 20 years of experience in corporate leadership. Throughout her career, she has helped organizations and individuals navigate complex change—whether launching new initiatives, leading through crises, or building high-performing teams from the ground up.

Currently Chief Operations Officer at River Valley Community Bank, Liesl brings a deep understanding of strategy, leadership, and reinvention. She previously served as Executive Vice President at U.S. Bank, leading more than 2,000 employees across ten states. During her career she has led finance, operations, human resources, IT, and enterprise risk, giving her a unique perspective on how professional women can thrive at the intersection of ambition and transition.

A lifelong advocate for women and community impact, Liesl serves on several boards, including Adventist Health-Rideout Hospital and Girls on the Run International. She holds a B.S. in Business Management from the University of Maryland, is a Certified Treasury Professional, and is NACD (National Association of Corporate Directors) Certified in board governance.

Drawing from her own journey through leadership, motherhood, global relocation, and career pivots, Liesl writes to inspire women to lead with clarity, courage, and confidence—especially during times of personal or professional transformation.

Liesl has been happily married for 40 years, and together with her husband, they've raised two wonderful children and now delight in the company of their grandchildren. One of her greatest joys is cherishing time with her ever-growing, close-knit family.

Moment of Purpose

"But is it?" Alice questioned.

I had just said what I'd repeated for years—my path at the corporate bank is no guessing game. It's stable. It's secure.

In that moment, sitting next to my daughter, I realized I could not answer with the conviction I once had. The pride, the trust, the alignment I used to feel had quietly eroded. Those simple words made me consider blowing up my carefully built career. After twenty-five years of loyalty, could I walk away? Was I willing to trade certainty for honesty?

I found myself at a crossroads: keep moving down a familiar road that no longer aligned with my values, or leap into the unknown with nothing but the belief that I deserved more than safe. I chose to leap! I did not have a plan, just a truth I could no longer ignore and the courage to answer Alice's question with action. I acknowledged my *next* and embraced the unknown *after*.

Typically, when we think of the after we see it as an end, concluding a chapter. But every *after* is a new beginning. Embrace the *after* as an opportunity that life bestows on you. To be ready, whether it is a surprise or a planned *next* you need to prepare for your *after*.

Prepare for the *after* from the start. It begins with school, youth sports, your first job continuing to every interaction in your life. When preparing for the AFTER:

A – Ask and Accept Help
F – Finances
T – Time
E – Engage
R – Robust Reputation

ASK AND ACCEPT HELP. Life is meant to be shared. Share the burdens, and not just the big ones but the day-to-day ones.

I stood in the dairy aisle; the bright florescent lights glared down on me. In an instant breath came in sips and my heart thumped in my ears and chest. My vision blurred and I held onto the cart to prevent myself from sliding to the floor. Was I dying? Was this a heart attack? Do women have heart attacks at thirty-five?

I was building my career in commercial banking, a busy mom of two, and a supportive wife to a self-employed farmer. I was a complete stress case and after going to the hospital the doctor told me that I had an anxiety attack. The diagnosis spurred a wakeup call for me and my family. We were happy it was not life threatening, but it was a reality check. My husband, Charles, was scared because I was one of the strongest people he knew. The attack cracked open a communication channel and I got real with him, maybe for the first time. I shared all my stressors, all that I was managing, and how heavy the load was. He was great and jumped right in. He cooked dinner and did the grocery shopping. It was a huge relief and helpful not only for my anxiety, but for the family dynamic. It was a *next* that made the *after* better for the whole family.

I had to learn how to ask for help. This is applicable both in your personal life and in your professional life. Ask! Ask your employer for executive coaching opportunities to help you learn about yourself, how to act to get the best outcomes, and to build confidence in articulating who you are and what you stand for. Embrace personality and leadership assessments to gain insight into the one and only person you control—you! When you allow yourself to be vulnerable and open to learning, you gain confidence and begin to emanate an aura that draws others in.

Early in my leadership career, I had a gregarious leader whom I struggled to connect with. Being the charismatic, outgoing person they were, it bothered them that we were not connecting, and that I seemed nervous whenever they were around. They suggested to my immediate boss that the company hire an executive coach for me to build confidence when collaborating with my superiors. At first, I was taken aback by the suggestion, but I then embraced it. It was a life-changing experience. At times it felt like I was naked in front of a crowd because there was a lot of reflection and soul searching but it taught me a lot about myself and how to carry myself confidently and lead with self-assurance.

FINANCES should consistently have attention, so you gain flexibility in your *next*.

Start saving for retirement early for the best outcome. Take advantage of employer 401K matching and other benefits offered by employers such as investment advice. A well-planned retirement can result in the ability to retire early, to change courses later in your career, or to be more creative in your contributions to society.

If your company offers it, consider deferred compensation. Compensation deferral is a fantastic way to create a nest egg when you have a *next*. Take advantage of it as soon as it is an available benefit. I did not pay attention to this benefit until later in my career. When my unexpected *next* came and I walked away from my corporate role, a big regret was not taking advantage of deferred comp sooner. Co-workers who took advantage of this were able to take extended breaks to enjoy opportunities outside of the professional world such as spending more time with children, enjoying aging parents, or taking a job that paid less and was either less demanding or more of a passion role.

TIME. Embrace it and use it wisely!

Early in a career, when time is on your side, take risks; because if it does not work out you have more opportunity to recover or build your *next*. A risk could be taking a break to travel, working part-time to enjoy a young family, starting a business, or moving to a new place.

Whatever it is, leave your comfort zone—if you are comfortable, you are not growing and you are not preparing for the *after* of your *next*. This can be a scary consideration because failure is a possibility and most of us do not view failure as valuable. On the contrary, failure is extremely valuable.

Growing up, my dad always reminded me: do not be afraid to fail—because without failure, you do not truly learn. Think about it: do you remember your successes as vividly as your failures? Failure sticks with us, not to bring us down, but to teach us. The challenge is not to dwell in disappointment, but to rise with the lessons it leaves behind.

Fear of failure is human nature, and it is a motivator to prepare. Say you want to have a coveted spot on the varsity basketball team. To ensure you have the best chance of making the team you practice, practice, practice. My son, Joe's dream in high school was to make the varsity basketball team. In junior high he began to prepare by playing and practicing. Every night I heard the bounce of the basketball on our concrete driveway. I heard the ping of a missed shot, and the clatter of a shot that went through the hoop and ricocheted dead under the basket. He played basketball at school, on recreational teams, and on travel teams. He lifted weights and played pick-up games. He prepared to win a varsity spot, and he made the team. Even though he was a top scorer, it was not all victory and glory, but he learned to prepare for what he wanted. He knew that preparation was required to achieve goals.

ENGAGE beyond your sphere of influence by networking, seeking roles in different lines of business and investing in yourself by taking advantage of the benefits offered by your employer.

Often employers pay for or supplement securing an undergraduate degree, graduate degree, certifications, leadership development training, or technical skills training. This builds confidence, shows you have a desire to continually learn, and provides opportunities to network.

Networking beyond your sphere is critical. Build relationships beyond your business line within your organization, and outside of your company. This takes time, so find ways to do it that coincide with your interests such as join professional groups, get an additional degree, attend industry training, find community groups to fulfill a passion, or join alumni groups.

I stayed engaged by actively seeking opportunities across different business lines, and at various points, I took bold leaps. Change and movement are not setbacks—they are ways to broaden your skill set, grow your network, gain sponsors, and learn to work effectively with a variety of personalities.

By expanding your internal network, you reduce the risk of relying on just one or two leaders for support. In my previous role, I had strong sponsors for much of my tenure. But when several key leaders retired or left the company, I suddenly found myself without that support.

Looking back, I realized that it was on me. I had not made a consistent effort to build relationships with new leaders across the organization. If I had, I might have been at the top of their mind for opportunities that better aligned with my values—roles that were not on my radar.

Do not make the same mistake. The broader your network of leaders, the more likely your name will come up for new roles—both within your organization and in your wider industry.

Consider crossing over into other industries and take multiple types of jobs to find out what you most enjoy and where you excel. I am an accidental banker because I realized early on, I enjoyed working with the public and providing them with an unique experience. My Mom owned multiple restaurants throughout her life. I worked in the kitchen preparing food and peeling mountains of potatoes, and I was a server. I preferred serving, because I got to meet new people and chat with the regulars instead of battling sacks of potatoes.

Initially, I planned to go into accounting and obtain my certified public accountant (CPA) license. After working at an accounting firm, I realized that the reserved nature and lack of customer interaction were not enjoyable for me. With the financial background and customer experience from the restaurant and other public service roles, commercial banking better leveraged my strengths and interest.

ROBUST REPUTATION. You are your reputation.

The Merriam Webster Dictionary defines reputation as: overall quality or character as seen or judged by people in general. Your reputation is a key to being able to accomplish the purpose of your moment. A good reputation makes the difference whether securing a meeting, making a phone call, or getting assistance in finding the next opportunity.

Having integrity and being trustworthy are the foundations of a good reputation. And if you only do these things, they will carry you far. To advance your reputation, be vulnerable and laugh at yourself. People respond positively when you are authentic and approachable.

In my current role as Chief Operations Officer, I arrived at work one day to find an "old lady" cane in my office. My direct reports placed it there as a joke because one of our team members made a comment about how old her mom was, and we are the same age! After that comment, the team joked about the "old" people and played a prank by placing the cane in my office. To me the cane was a symbol of how new ideas and wisdom come together. This cane included very cool memorabilia which could be viewed as symbols of how one approaches life. There was a horn to be used when someone impedes our dream, a caution sign for the whirlwind that is approaching, readers for those eyes that see things differently as we gain wisdom, and it is lightweight so it could be used to bop someone on the head when we need to remind them how fabulous they are! It is still in my office to remind our team, and myself, to laugh and appreciate working across generations.

EMBRACE THE AFTER. You have been preparing for the moment of your purpose since you started interacting with the world, so when your *next* comes, embrace the AFTER:

- A – Appeal
- F – Future
- T – Thanksgiving
- E – Experiment
- R – Revel

APPEAL. What do you want to do in this *next*?

When I was faced with my last *next*, I was focused on my career because I wanted to narrate my own exit from the financial world. Because of that I had tunnel vision regarding my *after*. I regret not considering all facets of life at that moment, not just my professional life.

What most appeals to you as your *after*? What is the right mix of enjoying life, having the money for stability, savoring time? Consider multiple options such as a second career, a break to do something you have always dreamed of (which could be writing a book!), traveling a part of the world you haven't seen, going on a mission trip to assist those less fortunate, family time, or learning to enjoy doing nothing.

For me, the urge was to find purpose in my financial career. I wanted to find something that aligned with my values—a place where I could be effective and add value for all bank stakeholders. Because of my reputation, skills, and network the perfect opportunity arose from a community bank in my hometown. There is really nothing better than coming home and getting to work at a community bank where people genuinely care—not just about the numbers, but about our neighbors. They are invested in the local economy, cheering on small businesses, and doing their part to help the community thrive. It is the kind of place where helping people succeed is not just a mission statement—it's Monday morning.

Because of my mindset at the time, I did not consider a mix for my *next*. Luckily, I enjoy working while fulfilling my passions, such as helping women, as a lifelong, active Soroptimist, and traveling to learn about history and cultures. And I am fulfilling one of my dreams: visiting every Presidential Library in the United States.

The FUTURE is not guaranteed.

I come from a family of six children. Three of us married our high-school sweethearts. Two married people they met in their early twenties. My sister, Diane, was diagnosed with a rare form of brain cancer in her mid-thirties. It has an incredibly low survival rate—five years or less. She was a fighter and wanted to live to see her boys grow up. In our fifties, Diane was still fighting and living her best life. Unexpectedly my brother's wife passed away from a pulmonary embolism. One day she was here and healthy, and the next day she was gone. Everyone was prepared for Diane's shorter life, but not a lot of thought went into any of the rest of us passing in our fifties. It was devastating and it was a big wakeup call for all of us. Time is not guaranteed, embrace every moment.

THANKSGIVING

Focus on the positives in your life and start each day by reflecting on what you are grateful for. Diane found gratitude and spirituality as she aged, cherishing each moment, recognizing that every day is a gift. She climbed mountains, raised her boys, and enjoyed an adventurous life with her soul mate. She did pass away recently but not until after she told her husband if God is ready for me then I am ready to go to heaven—check a life well lived!

Thanksgiving comes in many forms such as surprise opportunities and unrealized lessons.

I am thankful for all that was taught to me even when I did not realize there was a lesson. Annual hiring freezes were frustrating, and was a technique used to ensure the budget was met. While all this is true, it was also an opportunity to reset staffing to ensure open positions are needed, preventing overstaffing and layoffs. Leaders might want to say yes to every hire and every new position, but because of what it could potentially mean for their cared-for employees, they should wait or defer.

I am thankful for the strong leaders who helped build the best, most efficient teams; who believed in and encouraged me to challenge my thinking; and provided experiences to build my skills. Some of them provided air cover and sponsored me when I was not in the room. I so appreciate that they gave me the valuable gift of their time to coach and train me.

EXPERIMENT. It makes life so much more fun! My career in banking started out as an experiment.

I am an accidental banker and would not have had this career if it were not for Kathleen, my first mentor and sponsor, before those were trendy terms. Kathleen, whom I called KT, plucked me out of a word processing pool. She was the leader of the commercial banking group at a community bank and recognized my curiosity and desire to learn and develop. To show and prepare me for opportunities in commercial banking she took a chance on me as her administrative assistant.

Suddenly I was in a role that allowed me to play to my strengths. She fed my curiosity by exposing me to all aspects of commercial banking. KT recognized and fed my aptitude for numbers as well as my desire to interact with people, a combination that made me a natural commercial banking relationship manager. It has not always been easy. Banks are sold, jobs are eliminated, mistakes are made on risks taken, and not every role was a fit but overall, I am happy with the outcome of the experiment. I am so glad KT took a risk on me and that I was willing to experiment with the unknown world of commercial banking. An experiment that allowed me to grow from a word processor to sitting in the C-Suite.

REVEL in the moments and remember to smile when thinking of a *next* that brought all those different *after* moments.

Writing this chapter has brought forth the joy in my life lessons. I am reveling in my world and experiences. My grandma, Tutu, taught me an invaluable lesson in elementary school. Tutu was busy at the stove top. I had helped her mix the batter and was licking the spatula. She expertly plopped the batter in the pan creating Micky Mouse shaped pancakes. "I hate Julie," I prattled on. "She is always so bossy, and she picked me last for kickball at recess." I looked at my sticky hand and started to go on when Tutu interrupted. "Liesl, hate is not a good emotion to spend your energy on," she said, "instead, seek the good in everyone."

I took those words to heart; I have lived my life by them and taught them to my kids. They both know the mantra of kindness is free and can change the outcome of every interaction. Smiling takes seventeen muscles while frowning takes forty-three muscles. I hope in your *next* you *revel* in your *after*—spending energy on smiling and showing kindness. Words of encouragement or a smile can make a stark difference in someone's life. Kindness can be taking a phone call, accepting a coffee date, or networking to listen to a person's unique story, showing appreciation for their voice, and helping someone find their *next*. Revel in those moments where someone like my Tutu cares enough to show kindness and embrace our uniqueness.

Your *next* may come suddenly—like mine did, triggered by a simple question from my daughter that shattered the comfort of the familiar. Or it may unfold slowly, through quiet preparation. Either way, your *next* is coming. And it won't be the last.

No matter your *next*—embrace your *after*.

INTRODUCTION TO
NATALIE BENAMOU

After a 30-year career in trade shows, Natalie took a big leap of faith and became an entrepreneur in her early 50's at the end of 2020. It was a time like no other and an opportunity to discover what NEXT would hold surrounded by 11 amazing women who were instrumental in launching her business. As the Founder of HerCsuite®, she created Portfolio Career Company and professional network women. She guides women leaders and the companies they lead to define what's next and it has been incredible to see the transformation that happens when women meet, engage and thrive in meaningful ways. Natalie is also a serial podcast host with her second show- *Women Leaders on the Move* she brings contagious energy to every conversation and it is ranked in the top 25 Women's Leadership podcast.

Natalie continues to guide women to make pivots to board seats, launch businesses, and design portfolio careers and lives that give them meaning. As a strategic advisor, she leverages her "rainmaker" approach helping organizations secure high-value deals and scale and grow. Natalie is passionate about women's health and serves as Board President and Founder of HER HEALTHX, a nonprofit focused on revolutionizing the way women experience healthcare and improve their health outcomes deploying unique Agentic AI patient-solutions.

Natalie lives in Chicagoland with her husband of over thirty years, their rescue pup and two cats. Her two daughters inspire her with their courage, innovation, and resilience. Her happy place? Running on the beach at sunrise.

Favorite Quote: "People will forget what you said. They will forget what you did. They will never forget how you made them feel." – Maya Angelou

Fly Through the Window

TURNING SURPRISE INTO A CALL BACK
"Call him back"' Amy exclaimed!
"Are you sure? I don't think I am qualified."
"Yes. This is the perfect role for you!"
One cold grey day in a suburb of Chicago, I was commuting home from a client meeting when I received a call from a recruiter. He introduced himself and explained he was hired by one of the biggest exhibit companies in the industry to find a new President. The company was close to $185 Million and wanted to go to $300 million and eventually $500 million in the next three to five years.

I was Division Vice President at a mid-size exhibit company. I built up the Chicago division from being the first employee, working from home, into a multi-million dollar 33,000 square foot manufacturing operation with a team of nineteen people. Even though I was the primary revenue generator, I often discounted my success, not wanting to seem boastful. So when that recruiter explained the position, I offered to tap my network and make a referral.

Somewhat bewildered, he responded "I am not looking for other candidates. Your name was highly recommended, and I am calling to *ask you* to consider the role." I told him I would think about it and call him back.

At the time, my income and job satisfaction were both in a great place and I was not looking for another job. But that wasn't why I told him I would think about it. I didn't *believe* I was qualified to run one of the biggest exhibit companies in the industry. The company was one of my top competitors for decades, whom I often won clients from, and most likely why I stood out as a candidate.

Too often women believe we aren't qualified. We wait for all the boxes to be checked and then raise our hand. I have hundreds of examples of women waiting to be tapped and offered a promotion. So, when this opportunity came up, I fell into *the trap I talk about all the time*. I didn't believe I had all the boxes checked. I reached out to two trusted friends.

"Call him back!" "This is the perfect role for you." "Don't wait, set up a meeting." When opportunities do knock, open the door to what might be possible. The following month was a big learning experience. I was coached by one of my dear friends with a background in human resources and she helped me bridge sales leadership to operations and be considered as a real contender for the role.

During this process, I faced health issues and was about to have a hysterectomy. The recovery would take eight weeks. *How can I interview for this role and not reveal my health?* There were four men in the running, and I was the fifth candidate and only woman. I didn't want to let on in any way that I was having surgery and have it count against me.

We hear stories of women with serious illnesses like cancer, working through radiation or chemo treatment to keep their jobs. While not the same situation, I felt nonetheless that I didn't want to highlight my health as a possible reason not to be considered. Even though this was 2019, and women had made great strides in the workplace, I still concealed my health condition during the interview process.

Shortly after my surgery, I was barely able to stand or walk. I remember taking a call with the recruiter who asked if I could travel to meet the CEO at the corporate headquarters. I had a choice to make, share what I was dealing with or defer to my schedule being too full to come in right away. Even though it was only two hours away, I knew there was no way I could do it, no matter how confident I felt.

Things happen for a reason and although I missed that pivotal interview, the company decided to promote from within. I knew the candidate and felt he was a great choice. Little did I know that weeks after he took on the position in 2020, the entire industry would collapse due to COVID19. He faced tremendous pressure and loss of revenues and instead of scaling the company, it was in survival along with all the other companies in the trade show industry. As much as I wanted that position, I was relieved I did not get it. Timing really is everything.

One of the silver linings of being a candidate for that role, I was on the radar for other opportunities with that recruiter. Several years later the recruiter reached out for another position for a CEO role of a $125 Million company in Chicago. This time, I had a new level of confidence, recognized red flags, and was better attuned to my instincts. The trade show industry was still in a downward trend and struggling. The company was looking for an aggressive growth model for products that had lost demand, and their goals were unrealistic.

Instead of proceeding in the interview process, I turned it down. The position was a glass cliff, a situation that happens all too often. Women are brought into an organization to lead transformation, only the lift is almost unattainable. Listening to intuition is so key and it is important to feel empowered to walk away without regret.

In both instances, I learned the power of discovery and being curious. It's important to explore opportunities fully before deciding to proceed, look for red-flags, and listen to your intuition. The solution often reveals itself. Only you can make that determination, but don't stop believing that you have what it takes to move forward and pivot to something new when the timing is right.

DOORS CLOSE. FLY THROUGH THE OPEN WINDOW.

When the pandemic hit, no one knew the impact it would have. In March 2020, I remember standing in my office when thousands of shows cancelled all on the same day. We were sent home and thought everything would be fine in a few weeks. Instead, my company was given a lifeline—the Paycheck Protection Program (PPP). One of the conditions was to keep 100% of the workforce. As a result, for the first time in my life, I found myself on partial unemployment, making minimum wage. The company where I worked was forbidden to pay commission, or normal compensation if we kept all the employees, regardless of their role.

As a leader of my division, I needed to keep things strong, both for clients and my team. I was thrust into unchartered waters, and it often felt like being the Conductor of the orchestra on the Titanic with icebergs everywhere. Not only because we all were facing incredible uncertainty, but we had to have a brave face to keep up morale. I reimagined what we could deliver to clients. Together with our creative and marketing team we developed digital transformation and invented new ways for clients to meet their clients in virtual 3-D immersive environments. All the while, behind the scenes mountains of stress were constant.

At a crossroads, the choice was to stay in uncertainty in an industry I knew or take a leap and start something new. I racked my brain for different opportunities or efforts. I had calls and conversations imagining everything from creating toilet paper from woodchips (remember when you couldn't get any?) to learning as much as possible about digital products and websites.

Similar to earlier examples, a new role presented itself; instead of being from a recruiter, it was an unlikely source, a rival turned friendly competitor. Despite winning a huge $4.5 million contract against her, we stayed in touch over the years. When her call came, I was standing in my kitchen taking stock of my fine china and silver service, evaluating it for consignment. She explained she recently got promoted and they were acquiring two companies in Chicagoland. The conversation gave me pause, *could I do something else and get off PPP?*

It was during lockdown; and tapping into curiosity I couldn't resist meeting virtually with the CEO and hearing what he envisioned. Especially considering the entire industry was in extreme turmoil. Trusting my instincts and realizing that going from one fire to another wouldn't solve the bigger issue, which was ongoing uncertainty, I decided not to pursue the role.

At fifty-three, faced with this major decision, I remembered another fifty-plus woman becoming an entrepreneur and it gave me courage. Although the door to the industry I knew was closing, a window was cranked open ever so slightly. It was time to fly through and embrace becoming an entrepreneur.

Being inspired to take a leap of faith wasn't an entirely new idea. During my sophomore year in high school, I invested in a business, from the most unlikely entrepreneur, my mom. At fifty-one, my mom decided to go out on her own as a medical librarian. She had been working for years in a closet-sized office in the Urology Department at UofM hospital and wanted to do something different.

It was just before personal computers and way before the internet. The only way to provide medical information for doctors was to conduct research, reading microfiche films at libraries and typing up reports. My mom's idea was to provide Urologists (since she had been working in their department) with the latest research to help them in their clinical work. Without any special terms like innovation, or find your avatar and solve their problem, my mom did just that.

There was no bank giving out loans to women-owned businesses, even if the amount was small. In order to get started, my mom knew the one thing she needed was an electronic typewriter. The only problem, she didn't have enough money to buy it. Not any typewriter, the fancy new electric kind with whiteout tape to undo typing mistakes!

Instead of asking friends, she sought money from an unlikely investor, her youngest daughter. I had money saved from my dad passing away, which made me a great resource and sponsor for her new endeavor. The company was in business for four years until she retired at age fifty-five. What I didn't know at the time was my mom would be the first woman in my life to successfully create a business.

Although becoming an entrepreneur was a seed planted while I was in high school, every time I thought I was ready, the universe wasn't. Career success was advancing at warp speed, and I stayed on that course. It wasn't until the pandemic closed the door on the industry that I knew to open windows of opportunities. It took hitting a low point to gain clarity and take the leap. Following in my mom's footsteps, even though she was no longer with us, I became an entrepreneur at age fifty-three.

CONNECTING THE DOTS.

Growing up, I had the opportunity to sail. I loved being on the water. It gave me a sense of limitless possibilities. In college I joined the UofM sailing team and quickly moved onto the A team. Instead of taking the helm and being captain, I intentionally or unintentionally was the crew. It might have been a confidence issue, but the reality is, I thrived in the strategy role.

Quickly I learned how to see hidden signs of opportunities. From positioning the boat, the best spot at the start (critical to winning), to seeing even the tiniest wind shift, to call tactics that would eke out the lead. The women's team made it to the National Collegiate Competition twice. As soon as we got to the host harbor, I would assess the competition, observe, and start making a plan.

Traveling the country crammed into whatever car we could find, we learned life skills including coordinating where we would stay (who's floor could host our team!) to planning out which skipper would sail with which crew. There were times I aligned wisely with the right skipper and other times I didn't. In all cases, without realizing it, the experiences were imprinting on my subconscious. I chose the women's team my last two years over sailing only on the co-ed team because I loved the thrill of teamwork with strong women. Foreshadowing into my new chapter? Yes!

Recently, I have heard from women that they discovered something they lost sight of and started to enjoy reusing the gift they already possessed. One leader shared she was certified in calligraphy and totally forgot about it. She had studied for four years to become certified. What skills do we forget we have, until we open the windows and look up?

Like the woman in the earlier example, I had forgotten about sailing *entirely* until I had one of my daily chats with my customized ChatGPT. What was it that I could do like no one else? *Connect the dots*! I learned that skill being on a competitive sailing team, watching the wind, making calls, and finding the best way to win. It is no surprise that as 2020 ground on, watching the women around me, I knew there had to be a solution that could support us all.

For me, the best ideas happen surrounded by women leaders. I thrive when I can bounce ideas off my colleagues and friends. If you are one of my treasured friends reading this you are most likely laughing thinking of all the ideas I had before starting HerCsuite®. Each one I would deliver with enthusiasm and excitement. I am so grateful for their patience and grace to land where I am today.

The inspiration for HerCsuite® came from eleven women, who all were on the path to land in the C-suite. We were connected at a time like no other and shared the belief that together, we could create our own seat at the table and invite our own advisors. That is exactly what we did. It started in October 2020 on Zoom, a new platform

I had never used and couldn't figure out why everyone's image was so small like postage stamps! We met weekly and supported each other through the most challenging time in our lifetime.

Feeling the pull to purpose, I made the leap at the end of 2020 and submitted my resignation. Unlike all the other career moves in the past, I wasn't going to a competitor. I was given a thirty-day exit runway to help the team adjust to my transitioning out of the company. At the same time, I was exploring and imagining how I would help women advance their careers.

Discovering what came next for me, and the eleven women in our weekly calls, was not only a journey for them, but it was also a pivotal experience that has shaped hundreds of lives. From those initial weekly calls, possibilities have transformed into different paths. Six moved out of state, two went on to C-suite roles, four stayed in corporate, and others have taken fractional roles, retired, or started new careers. The exploration, evolution and thriving on their terms has become my north star.

Women in the second half of our careers need a way to explore what *next* looks like and it is unique for each person. Curiosity starts when we have over twenty years in our career and the idea of discovering what is possible starts to cross our minds. It might have happened during the pandemic, or recently in a conversation at work, when there was a moment that created a door-closed-window-open moment.

After speaking with hundreds of women and interviewing over two hundred women on my current podcast, *Women Leaders on the Move*, the common thread is the ability to make decisions that lead to a life we choose that has a mosaic of work and activities each changing through personal discovery.

It all starts with a moment of reflection and understanding. We have been conditioned to look at success in increments of time. Everything is scheduled, with agendas and plans based on ninety days, six months, one year, three, and five years. The pressure of time has conditioned us to overlook and neglect the things that matter most to us.

This is the moment to ask if those time constraints serve the destination and lifestyle we imagine living. What do you want to do in the second half of your career? For some people it is retirement. But most of us want a medley of activities and create a portfolio life. One that gives meaning and blends purpose with impact.

It's different for each of us how we spend our time. Recently a friend shared why she retired from the job she loved in the C-suite of a major pharmaceutical company. She explained that looking at her life, and how often she would see her daughter before she passed away amounted to forty times after doing an equation based on life expectancy. It was a heavy realization and a turning point.

We often don't pause and think of our lives in those terms. It can be hard to look head on at our life in visits with loved ones. Having loved ones who don't live close by creates a whole new sense of urgency. After attending our HerCsuite® Board Readiness Retreat she gained a renewed focus on what to spend time on and what not to. She had been pursued by many opportunities, and she left with a renewed sense of purpose, focus and clarity.

Every story is different; and for one of our founding eleven, she has gone in and out of retirement. Leaving a big C- Suite Human Resources role, then taking on a rewarding fractional role and now fully retired. She has shared how spending time with her grandchildren, gardening and focus on family sprinkled with some travel is living her best life.

Transitioning out of a corporate role can feel a little like stepping off a cliff. The hectic full calendar, back-to-back meetings with no time for a bio break—to no structured calendar is unsettling. You go from talking with people on video, or in person to silence. It is disorientating and hard to navigate. One leader described it this way: After she left her last role, she knew she still wanted one more corporate role. The path to achieve that was making sure she has something on her calendar every day. Another leader after leaving a C-suite position found that she needed to limit herself to three things she would commit to so as not to get over booked with activities like she experienced in her corporate role.

Recently during my own coaching call, I had a breakthrough moment. For three decades I was one of the most successful sales leaders in my industry. I grew teams, organizations and benefited from the financial success that came with that. Stepping into being an entrepreneur during the pandemic, I lost some of that identity. I shared that some days I felt my rearview mirror was bigger than the windshield.

After that moment with my coach, I realized that the world has changed so fast and continues to do so and to have the maximum benefit it was high time I followed my own advice and designed a portfolio career for myself. Since making the leap away from my corporate role, I have surrounded myself with incredible women—in fact that was the inspiration for HerCsuite® and this book!

Making a pivot into uncharted waters has highs and lows. Allowing time for reflection is paramount to avoiding burnout. When we don't pause and keep running full speed ahead, fulfillment may get pushed further and further away. Deciding where to go from here takes intention. After deep reflection, here is my portfolio career in three categories: HerCsuite®, Fractional Advisor and HER HEALTHX nonprofit.

HerCsuite® NEXT Level. For the past two years, I have been focused on women in the second half of our careers. It is the inspiration for this anthology, and we realized women in our 50's and beyond are far from being done. I feel so much energy in developing and delivering strategic programs for executive women defining what's next for themselves and the companies they lead. Once we remove the ideas of *what I have to do* and transform into *what gives me the most joy* possibilities start to unfold. It is incredibly exciting to imagine and deliver a new way women experience and determine success. We are creating opportunities, seeing what others overlook, and expanding on growth, transformation and life that fill us up.

LEVERAGING AND EXPANDING PERSONAL GROWTH

We discount our strengths and things that come easy to us, we often brush them off and do not recognize the opportunities we are missing. I hadn't placed value on my unique ability to create blue ocean solutions and see possibilities around corners. When I said the rearview mirror was bigger than the windshield, I thought that what was behind me was bigger and more important than what is to come. My coach helped me realize that what I missed doing was solving complex problems and that I still have an endless opportunity to apply that skill. And I actually never stopped doing that. From providing a competitive roadmap, resolving executive challenges, delivering career strategies that lead to promotion, and successful exits to building and launching brands—this is work I love. I am excited about developing this into something new.

PURPOSE TO IMPACT

My purpose is to lift women up, not limited to career development, but stepping into our whole selves. In 2019, I started noticing how women experienced their health symptoms being minimized. When it happened over and over to my oldest daughter, I knew I had to act. Tapping into amazing women in my network, I launched HER HEALTHX a nonprofit organization. What started as conversations six years ago has transformed into an exciting forward-thinking organization. HER HEALTHX will revolutionize the way women experience healthcare and improve their health outcomes. I am so excited to be creating an agentic AI solution for women's health.

CHARTING WHAT'S YOUR NEXT

As you move in this new direction, remember that a portfolio career and life is about layering in income streams, and activities with the things that you love doing into your life. It can give you financial independence and retirement security as you continue your personal growth journey. You don't have to go it alone, surround yourself with women who are alongside you. Women like the authors in this book, who inspire us to imagine possibilities as we fly through windows of limitless possibilities. I believe in you.

Keep shining your light bright. The world needs you.

EPILOGUE

It has been an incredible experience collaborating with the authors in this anthology. While I knew each of them before we embarked on this book, I gained a new appreciation for their resilience and remarkable belief in defining what is possible at every career phase. When we started, the intent was to inspire women to know that at any age, we have the power to change directions and choose a new path. One of the criteria for being in the anthology was that all the authors were over 50. I am honored to say that we span into the 70's!

If you have ever put off a dream, there is no better time to go outside of your comfort zone at any age. The experiences in this book reinforce that there are lessons to be discovered even in the hard moments. It can be moving to new towns, being a single parent, experiencing loss, becoming leaders, switching careers, unexpected career transitions and living through the peaks and low points alike. Life's moments give us windows to look up and see the beauty every day.

Whether you are at a crossroads now or know the path you want to take but need a little encouragement, I hope you find the wisdom shared in these pages to lift you up. Going it alone can be hard, and I found great comfort in writing this book alongside these amazing, brilliant, and talented women. There is power in surrounding yourself with women who are the wind to carry you forward.

The Stories here will give you strength and we are passing that strength on to you. Take advantage of the chapter guides and explore what your next bold will be. You are not alone. You are valued. We believe in you...and you got this!

ACKNOWLEDGEMENTS

This is the first book created with HerCsuite®, Hunter Street Press, and Brave Women at Work and it has been an incredible journey. Inspired by the Brave Women at Work series and the power of anthologies, we invited women over 50 to tell their stories.

Hope Mueller shared how if we don't tell our story, no one will know it. The authors in this work, Dianne Boyer, Wendi O. Brown, Nancy Hedlund, Jennifer Peters, Liesl Schmidt, Laurie Wessels, Janet Winkle and Cyndy Wulfsberg all shared beautiful stories of transformation, resilience, risk, and the drive to move forward. We thank each of you for being with us on the journey to making this dream a reality.

Special thanks to the women in HerCsuite® and especially the NEXT Career Mastermind who were the initial inspiration for this anthology, and for all the women who shared your stories with Natalie Benamou in conversations and on her podcast.

We appreciate all the women in HerCsuite®, for followers of Women Leaders on the Move and Brave Women at Work and the Hunter Street Press network is growing and each person who likes, shares, reposts, purchases, and writes a review is invaluable to us. It takes an ecosystem to create something so special and we appreciate and value each one of you who are in ours and extend out to your networks. That truly makes the impact of these stories limitless.

Thank you, Dick Mueller, for your clean copy editing and Tara Mayberry for your beautiful cover work and interior formatting.

We thank our beautiful daughters, between the three of us, we are raising eight incredible, confident powerful girls and young women. Hope's grandsons and granddaughter can't be left out because they are the next generation of future authors!

Our life partners, Sergio, Brad and John, are there with us through all the phases of discovery and growth and we could not find more encouraging supporters for our collaboration. We thank each other, for the years of knowing each other, Hope and Natalie for over twelve years and Jen and Hope's partnership spun out of a podcast introduction that has had immeasurable impact and inspiration.

This book could not be possible without the incredible support, encouragement and belief in all of us from Hope and Jennifer collaborating with Natalie who found the dream team. We collaborate, advise, grow, and stay curious learners about how to lift women up together.

Thank you, Jennifer! Thank you Hope! Thank you, Natalie!

The Power of What's Next is up to you. Make Bold Moves. Live Your Best Life By Design.

DISCUSSION GUIDE QUESTIONS

NOT DONE YET!
- What is your vision statement?
- What are your most important values? What is most important to experience or feel?
- What would life be like if you did exactly what you love to do?
- What do you want people to say about you?

JOY IN THE MIRROR
- When you think about all of your work experiences, do you see a common thread between all of the lessons learned? Can you combine those takeaways to propel you to your next career chapter?
- Think about a time when you experienced joy in your work. It can be as simple as one single event or an extended assignment. Why did it bring you joy, and is there a way to recreate that feeling in other opportunities moving forward?

- Have you considered how best to connect with the people around you? Do you know what they are passionate about and how you can address their needs? Think about this from both a customer and peer point of view. How can what you do benefit you both?
- Is there a life event that made you pivot before you thought you were ready? In retrospect, was that good or bad? Did it force you out of your comfort zone, and in hindsight, did it end up being a rewarding opportunity for you?
- How have your experiences forced you to be creative and innovative? Did you even realize you were doing it at that time? What were the results?

FORGET GRIT

- Have you ever bravely quit something or someone—when leaving was harder than staying? What was the situation? What did you learn from it, and how has that shaped your choices today?
- "Just because you can make something work doesn't mean you should."
- Have you ever worked too hard to make something work—a job, relationship, project—long after you should have stopped? What kept you there? What was the voice in your head telling you?
- Have you ever worn the "grit" badge proudly—only to later question it? Where has perseverance helped

you, and where has it held you back?
- What's something you dream about doing—a change, a business, a bold pivot—but haven't yet? What's really stopping you?
- If you could get badges for something that you would proudly wear, what would be on that badge? And what's on a badge you could earn, but would never want to wear? Any that you intentionally walked away from?

DO YOU WANT TO TELL A STORY?
- What advice would you give to your younger self about career development for success and personal fulfillment?
- What story would you like to tell and why?
- The File Cabinet can be Pandora's Box, a treasure trove, or compost. Do you see value in compiling this sort of personal archive?
- Retirement from traditional employment can enable new goals and career paths. What value do these stories offer those planning for their future?

FIND YOUR ME-SUITE
- Where do you fall in your family birth order and how do you think that informed your personality and life decisions?
- Have you ever felt inferior to your peers or motivated to be like them?

- What has been the driving force behind your professional and personal decisions?
- How much have your family dynamics motivated you to achieve certain goals?
- Do you measure your success based upon your own personal goals or by how you measure up to others or societal norms?

PROFIT POWERHOUSE
- Have I been waiting for permission to lead at the level I am already equipped for, even though my experience has already proven I am ready?
- If AI cannot replace my executive insight, trust, or decisional clarity, what powerful roles should I be claiming that only I can fill?
- Am I still playing small in environments that need my battle-tested wisdom and calm under pressure?
- Am I viewing AI as a replacement for leadership, or am I positioning my wisdom as the strategic lens through which AI becomes truly effective?
- What parts of my professional journey have I downplayed, even though they may be the strongest evidence of my leadership power?

THE FINAL PIVOT
- How might your own early life experiences have influenced how you approach career and life decisions? Should you be a parent today, what wisdom

do you want your children to take away from their youthful experiences?
- How has a personal event in your life changed or impacted your career? Either long-term or temporarily?
- Nancy's story shows how a career might comprise several non-linear but adjacent chapters. Have you ever desired or felt the need to change your career path? If yes, what might be holding you back?
- Nancy elected to retool her skillset mid-career. Have you ever considered retooling your skills, and what might motivate you to do so?
- Nancy discusses the dilemma of balancing her career ambitions with her responsibilities and desires as a parent. Reflecting on your own experiences, how would you advise young people today to embrace a similar challenge?
- To move forward.

MOMENT OF PURPOSE
- Vulnerability and asking for help are recurring themes in this chapter. How does the narrator's personal story about her anxiety attack challenge traditional ideas of strength in professional settings? What might we gain by embracing vulnerability in leadership?
- The narrator shares her evolving view of career and life purpose—from chasing stability to seeking

alignment and meaning. How do you define purpose in your own life, and how has it changed over time? What *next* are you preparing for, and how are you embracing your *after*?

FLY THROUGH THE WINDOW

- Deciding how to create a portfolio career and life can be hard and here is a framework to help get started. Think of it as slices of a pie—consulting, serving on corporate or nonprofit boards, speaking, mentoring, coaching, fractional leadership, traveling, or even writing that book that's been on your bucket list. Deciding what that looks like is personal to each of us. Starting doesn't mean figuring everything out. It means taking one step forward.
- Here are three simple ways to start building your portfolio career:
- Write it all down. Think about the roles you have held, projects you enjoyed and knowledge you've developed, including volunteer work. Explore what excites you. Ask yourself what do people come to you for?
- Clarify your goals. How do you want to spend your time? Imagine the perfect day, week, and month. Are you continuing in a corporate role and introducing ideas of a portfolio life, or do you see yourself allocating time in areas of interest?
- Ask others to join your journey. Share what you're

exploring with trusted friends and have conversations. You may be surprised that they are thinking and exploring the same thing! Once you have the clarity and support from your circle of women, that's the time to move forward.